MW00446173

RETHINKING

MICHIGAN

INDIAN

HISTORY

RETHINKING
MICHIGAN
INDIAN
HISTORY

Patrick Russell LeBeau

Michigan State University Press • *East Lansing, Michigan*

Copyright © 2005 by Patrick Russell LeBeau
Reproduction rights granted for single-classroom use only. All other rights reserved.

⊗ The paper used in this publication meets the minimum requirements
of ANSI/NISO Z39.48–1992 (R 1997) (Permanence of Paper).

 Michigan State University Press
East Lansing, Michigan 48823-5245

Printed and bound in China.

10 09 08 07 06 05   1 2 3 4 5 6 7 8 9 10

LIBRARY OF CONGRESS CATALOGING-IN-PUBLICATION DATA
LeBeau, Patrick Russell, 1958–
Rethinking Michigan Indian history / Patrick Russell LeBeau.
p. cm.
SBN 0-87013-712-3 (pbk. : alk. paper)
1. Indians of North America—Michigan—History—Sources. 2. Indians of North America—
Michigan—Historiography. 3. Indians of North America—Study and teaching—Michigan.
4. Michigan—Historical geography. I. Title.
E78.M6.L43 2005
977.4004'97—dc22
2005009076

TEACHER CONSULTANTS / EDITORS
Susan E. Luter (Grand Ledge Public Schools)
Cynthia D. Scarlett (Okemos Public Schools)
Jennifer A. Cuthbert (Graphics/Collages)

MAPS
James Mitchell, Illustrator
Mike Lipsey, Cartographer
Patrick and Caitlin LeBeau

 In part, this book is made possible by a grant from the Michigan Humanities
Council (an affiliate of the National Endowment for the Humanities), 119 Pere
Marquette Dr., Suite 3B, Lansing, Michigan 48912-1280; (517) 372-7770;
www.mihumanities.h-net.msu.edu

Cover and interior design by Sharp Des!gns, Inc., Lansing, MI

g green press INITIATIVE   Michigan State University Press is a member of the Green Press Initiative and is
committed to developing and encouraging ecologically responsible publishing
practices. For more information about the Green Press Initiative and the use of recycled paper in
book publishing, please visit *www.greenpressinitiative.org.*

Visit Michigan State University Press on the World Wide Web at: *www.msupress.msu.edu*

DEDICATION

This book is dedicated to Rainbow Woman, Moon Light Walker, Rattling Sky Woman, and those other women who seek truth and spiritual knowledge. Leona Marie Wilkie and Herbert Paul LeBeau spent their whole lives sharing the many lessons contained in this book with anyone who would take the time to listen. This book is dedicated to them as well.

Contents

Acknowledgments xi

Introduction

Rethinking Michigan Indian History 1

Questioning 2

How to Use This Book

Lesson Organization and Format of Lessons 5

Historical Overview and Vocabulary

Overview 7

Vocabulary 8

Pretest

How Do We Know What We Know? 11

What Is the Purpose of a Pretest? 11

Procedures for Teachers 12

Answers to P-2 and Exploring Ideas 12

Questions for Thought and Discussion 13

Appended Resources 14

LESSON THE FIRST

Defining Our Terms and Exploring Stereotypes: Building a Specific Context

Major Premise 21

Objectives 21

Narrative 21

Activities 25

Appended Resources 29

LESSON THE SECOND

Challenging the "Great Man" Theory of History

Major Premise 41

Objectives 41

Narrative 41

Vocabulary: The Fallacy of the "Great Man" Theory of History 43

Short Biographies of Pontiac and Tecumseh 43

Short Biographies of Andrew Blackbird and Leopold Pokagon 44

Part 1: Warriors and Wars: Pontiac and Tecumseh 47

Part 2: Leopold Pokagon and Andrew Blackbird in the 1800s 50

Part 3: Historical Juxtapositions: Three Fires People in the Civil War . . . 54

Appended Resources 56

LESSON THE THIRD

Indian Treaties and the U.S. Constitution

Major Premise 77

Objectives 77

Narrative 78

Vocabulary 79

Important Concepts I 80

Important Concepts II 82

Treaty Rights and the U.S. Constitution Timeline (3.1) 82

Part 1: Sovereignty of Tribal Governments 83

Part 2: Indian Treaties as Supreme Law of the Land:

Article 6, Paragraph 2, U.S. Constitution 86

Part 3: Negotiating an Indian Treaty 88

Part 4: Tribes, States, and the U.S. Government: Treaty Rights

Lost and Won Back 92

Part 5: Indian Treaties: Exploring a Real Treaty 95

Appended Resources 96

LESSON THE FOURTH

How Historical Maps Influence Thinking about Michigan's Indians

Major Premise 131

Objectives 131

Narrative 132

Part 1: Location of Indian Land in the State of Michigan 136

Part 2: Relationships and Movement within Places: Michigan's
    Indians Interacting with the Michigan Landscape and
    Environment and the Influence of Indian Place-Names 145

Part 3: How Michigan's Land Cession Treaties and Indian
    Reservations Create Unique Regions within the State 151

Part 4: Different Ways of Mapping Culture and History 155

Appended Resources 160

Resources 162

Selected Instructional/Research Resources for Teachers 213

Acknowledgments

I am grateful to LuAnn Kern, former assistant director of the Michigan Humanities Council. She deserves special acknowledgment, for without her help and advice, the writing of this book would not have been possible. I am also grateful to the staff of the department of Writing, Rhetoric, and American Cultures at Michigan State University and to department chair Dr. Doug Noverr for assistance and counsel. Special thanks to Helen Hornbeck Tanner, Senior Research Fellow at the Newberry Library, for reading the manuscript and offering helpful suggestions and revision ideas. I am indebted to her for her time and efforts, though any mistakes in the text are, of course, mine.

The Marquette Mission Park and Museum of Ojibwa Culture in St. Ignace deserves special acknowledgment for use of the Ojibwa Migration Chart and supporting materials; similarly, the Detroit Public Library kindly permitted the use of the image of Payson Wolfe. Many thanks to the group of Native American teachers with whom I have spent hours discussing ways of teaching the complexities of Native American studies. They are the true source for the techniques and lessons contained in this book.

Special thanks to James Mitchell for the wonderful maps he produced and for all his advice and help on historical questions and clarifications. He has been an inspiration and a good friend for many years. Mike Lipsey, cartographer at the Center for Remote Sensing and Geographic Information Science, and the Atlas of Michigan Project deserve special thanks for assistance and preparation of the maps James Mitchell did not create.

Thanks to Jennifer A. Cuthbert for assistance in the creation of the collages not created by students and for assistance in the graphic design of the handouts.

Introduction

RETHINKING MICHIGAN INDIAN HISTORY

As the title suggests, this book encourages readers to rethink Michigan Indian history and to examine and challenge what they already know (or think they know) about Indians. Although each chapter begins with a historical/contextual essay, this is not a history book. It does not "correct" Michigan Indian history as much as serve as a guide to expand most students' knowledge of Michigan's Indians. This volume does not invalidate existing histories but instead asks readers to become critical thinkers and make conclusions. Through lessons and activities that stimulate the exploration of their opinions and ideas, students of American Indian history develop new perspectives about the nature of American Indian history in Michigan.

Although *Rethinking Michigan Indian History* focuses on Michigan, the themes and issues raised and investigated in each lesson are applicable and adaptable to other regions of the United States and Canada. The book can serve as a model where the specifics of state, tribe, and treaties are interchangeable. At a very basic level, the book seeks to teach the complexities of Indian history, culture, and contemporary issues in a simple and straightforward manner.

Rethinking Michigan Indian History seeks to foster a basic understanding of the subject by encouraging students to read analytical and narrative history in a critical manner. Readers will be asked to evaluate the reliability and truth value of histories, documents, and other primary and secondary sources of information.

Rethinking Michigan Indian History provides tools and resources to aid in the examination of what readers already know about Michigan Indian history and to identify and understand the sources of that information. Students examine primary sources such as the images of Indians used in the packaging of consumer products. Students analyze secondary sources, such as biographies of Indian warriors written by historians, and test the conclusions made by authorities such as historians and examine the way such sources teach about Indians. The lessons and activities direct readers to take another look at Indian history. How (and why) is Indian history presented and taught? Readers are directed to make observations and to gather evidence, enabling them to draw their own conclusions from data and sources they can easily obtain and examine.

Though readers are asked to think for themselves, this book builds from four conclusions the author has made from the same data to be explored by readers. Though the book is predicated on the idea that most readers will arrive at the same conclusions, the lessons are organized as a testable body of knowledge so that teachers and students can experiment, observe, examine, and reject or confirm the hypothetical conclusions that follow:

- Stereotypical representations of Michigan's Indians are what most people of Michigan understand and recognize.
- The U.S. Constitution protects and upholds Michigan Indian treaty rights.
- Michigan's Indians are alive and well in the modern world and are not artifacts of the past.
- Michigan's Indians change and adapt to circumstances and events; therefore, they are not frozen in any one image or time period.

QUESTIONING

Should you use the noun *Indian* or *Native American?* When you begin to look around American consumer culture, why do so many images of Indian themes, profiles of warriors, or Indian princesses adorn the wrappers and packaging of commercial products? Why can Indian tribes operate casinos and bingo halls? Why do a few Indian youths qualify for free tuition at some of Michigan's colleges and universities? Specifically, why do we ask these questions, and how do these questions influence our understanding of all Indians and specifically of Indians living in Michigan in both the past and the present? This book encourages readers to answer these and many more questions by interpreting observations and readings from a variety of sources.

Through a visual demonstration of the power of stereotypes to influence thinking and by a careful exploration of the connection between Indian treaties and the U.S. Constitution, *Rethinking Michigan Indian History* challenges the way Native American history and culture is taught from fourth grade through adult classrooms. Although teachers may pick and choose activities to augment their curricula, the book's chapters, hereafter referred to as *lessons*, are designed to be investigated in order:

- LESSON THE FIRST describes the influence of stereotypical images of Indians in American culture and the power of such images to distort understandings of Native American people and culture. Although the book is targeted at fourth-graders through adult learners, second- and third-graders are capable of exploring this lesson.
- LESSON THE SECOND explores how biography, especially the focus on "great men" of American Indian history, shifts the historical focus away from Indian families and communities to heroic deeds, warfare, and killing.

Students in fourth and fifth grade who study biographies will find this lesson a useful addition.

- LESSON THE THIRD demonstrates the U.S. Constitution's power to guarantee and protect Michigan Indian sovereignty and treaty rights. The relationship between Indian treaties and the U.S. Constitution explicates four basic concepts about Indian treaty rights: (1) sovereignty, (2) reserved rights, (3) goods and services bought and paid for, and (4) money owed to Indian peoples for ceded lands. Units on U.S. government can add to the discussion and critical issues raised in this lesson.

- LESSON THE FOURTH investigates the way historical and contemporary maps tell a story of U.S. history and how states are created. Many maps overlook reserved rights and original landownership by Michigan's Indians. This lesson addresses the five themes of geography from a new perspective.

How to Use This Book

In *Rethinking Michigan Indian History*, each chapter (or lesson) contains three sections: (1) a narrative introduction; (2) activities, including extensions and connections to sources or activities found outside the context of the book; and (3) appended photocopy-ready 8½" × 11" handouts and resources. The introduction gives context, background, and essential information. The activities are ready-to-use lesson plans for classroom implementation. The resources are carefully designed handouts for student use, meant for the activities, but also usable in any way teachers or students devise. Therefore, the book is intended as a self-contained body of resources for students of American Indian history without requiring any further research or gathering of information.

The appended resources for each lesson are collected in an appendix to the lesson for easy access. In the text, references to "Appended Resources" appear as citations within parentheses. The two resources in the pretest section are numbered P-1 and P-2, while the resources in the lesson sections are numbered identifying the lesson number followed by a handout number (e.g., 1.1, 1.2, 2.1).

The design of *Rethinking Michigan Indian History* is also modular, meaning that each lesson can be used whole or in part. Students need not follow the lessons in the order presented, although this arrangement allows for a more comprehensive coverage and reading of Michigan Indian history. Conversely, teachers can pick and choose any piece, no matter how small or large, of a lesson and integrate it into their curricula. This guide and resource are intended to be as friendly, flexible, and usable as possible.

Along these lines, photocopy rights are freely given for any educational purpose. All handouts/resources in the appended sections are ready for photocopying: make as many copies as you wish, but please keep the copyright line, © Patrick Russell LeBeau 2005/All Rights Reserved, on all copies.

LESSON ORGANIZATION AND FORMAT OF LESSONS

Lessons 1–4 are complete units divided into three distinct sections. The lessons are called "Lesson the First," "the Second," "the Third," and "the Fourth" because many Indian treaty articles are also labeled as such (e.g., Article the First). Each lesson begins with the narrative and presents methods of analysis in the form of questions, re-examination of standard historical forms, and explication of difficult concepts. The narrative often includes information and definitions repeated in the activities and appended resources sections. Teachers can photo-copy important concepts, definitions, and information from the appended resources without having to include the entire narrative.

The second section of each lesson provides a set of activities and exercises designed to further explore the ideas and issues laid out in the narrative section. The activities include questions for thought and discussion, topics for short papers, and suggestions for research and reading. Objectives are stated and ideas for preparation are given. Then, a series of classroom activities are presented in a step-by-step approach.

Each lesson concludes with appended resources, a set of copy-ready student handouts and other reproducible resources for that particular lesson. The appended resources include graphic organizers, transparencies, prepared hand-outs, and visual aids such as maps, timelines, and collages. These resources are designed to supplement discussions and writing assignments.

In each lesson, the narrative and activities sections reference the appended resources section by lesson and handout number. This is also how they are listed on the CD-ROM.

Historical Overview and Vocabulary

OVERVIEW

The leading actors of this book are the Chippewas, the Ottawas, and the Potawatomis, who lived and still live within the boundaries of what we now call the state of Michigan. However, historical and legal documents, including the U.S. Constitution, also play major roles in this study. The time period is necessarily narrowed to 1760 through the present. Ancient Indian mound builders, other historical Indian populations that resided for a time in the state (such as the Hurons/Wyandots) as well as present-day Indian people, like the author, who find themselves living in the state as a result of marriage or jobs, must necessarily take a minor role in this book. To explain a bit further the narrowing of the scope of the text, long before 1760, the Hurons were a major Michigan Indian population but by 1760 were reduced to a remnant and landless population. (Also, the Nottawaseppi Huron Band of Potawatomi Indians, named after the Huron River, should not be mistaken as Hurons). The Wyandots held a reservation at Flat Rock, on the Huron River, when Michigan became a state; however, due to historical circumstances not to be covered in this text, the Wyandots' reservation was terminated. This book focuses on federally recognized Indian tribes and those Michigan tribes that have signed treaties with the U.S. government. These groups form the universe of this brief and specific yet critical and thorough exploration of four categories of historical investigation.

At the beginning of the twenty-first century, Michigan's Native American population is comprised of the indigenous People of the Three Fires, some remnant Hurons and Wyandots, as well as people of many other Native American nations who have moved here for economic reasons. The Chippewas constitute the second-largest tribal group in North America, with bands throughout the Upper Midwest and Canada. In Michigan, the Chippewas originally lived in the eastern half of the Lower Peninsula and most of the Upper Peninsula. The Ottawas originally lived in the western half of the Lower Peninsula on lands from the Straits of Mackinaw south to St. Joseph. The Potawatomis originally lived in southwest and central Lower Michigan. Today, Michigan's Native American people continue to live on or near their traditional homes as well as in Michigan's urban centers.

Within the United States, Michigan's Chippewas (Ojibwas), Ottawas (Odawas), and Potawatomis comprise one of the ten largest Native American populations, and are commonly referred to as the People of the Three Fires. Teachers and students should know that the term, People of the Three Fires, is a recent 20th-century innovation, not appearing in any treaties or literature earlier, but is used here as a way of speaking of them as a whole. Michigan's Native Americans occupy land and territories throughout the state and have distinct cultures. They have federally recognized tribal governments and reservations. All of these tribes have signed formal treaties with the U.S. government; consequently, the tribes have special reserved rights and privileges as citizens of tribal governments. The formality of treaties recognizes the indigenous status of these particular Native American people.

VOCABULARY

Although many terms and words are defined within the body of the text, two require special attention.

Indigenous

Indigenous is defined as existing, born, or produced naturally in a land or region. If you are indigenous to Michigan, then you were born and you exist (live) in the state. When applied to Native Americans, the term also means "original inhabitants," the permanent residents of a particular region. Indigenous Indians are the people with whom the federal government signed treaties (that is, entered into agreements) and are consequently the people recognized as the original landowners for such purposes as land transfers and acquisitions. Many Three Fires people are indigenous to Michigan in this sense.

Federally Recognized / Degree of Indian Blood

Federally recognized is a term referring to the legal status of Indian tribes and individual Native Americans and their relation to the federal government.

Any tribes that have signed treaties with the United States or can prove indigenous residency in a particular land base are, or may be, federally recognized. Federal recognition also means that a tribe (for example, the Saginaw Chippewa Indian Tribe) has reserved a portion of land for members' specific use. On that land, the tribe can form a government and function like any local (city, township, or county) or state government. Tribes can also set standards for tribal membership, inclusive and/or outside of federal standards of recognition.

When an individual Native American is federally recognized, he or she has (1) met a federal standard of degree of Indian blood (DIB) in a particular tribe and/or (2) is an enrolled member of a tribe that has signed a treaty with the United States. DIB means that the Native American in question is a descendant of a Native American person or family on the federal registry of Native

Americans and belongs to a tribe recognized by the federal government. (Note: It is possible to be 100% Indian heritage, but not have sufficient DIB in any single tribe to qualify for membership.) For the most part (but not always), the person must be of at least ¼ Indian blood. This is verifiable by blood audit. For example, if a person can prove that one grandparent is 100 percent Native American, then that person can claim federal recognition with or without tribal membership. Tribal membership, however, does not necessarily depend on DIB or federal recognition. Tribes make their own rules and requirements for membership.

Federal recognition is important and distinctive because only federally recognized tribes and Native American people can benefit from federal services, privileges, rights, monies, and promises made and guaranteed by treaties and the U.S. Constitution. Tribal standards follow or expand this basic tenet of DIB; tribes can—and do—provide services and rights to members regardless of federal standards.

Not all Native Americans (¼-blood to full-blood) are necessarily federally recognized. As a result of many historical circumstances beyond the scope of this text, many people cannot prove their DIB; therefore, they are not federally recognized. This does not mean, however, that they have no status as Native Americans. Families, communities, and tribes (as described earlier) have often extended recognition to individuals that these groups deem qualified as Native American.

Pretest

HOW DO WE KNOW WHAT WE KNOW?

At times, our knowledge is a mystery. Students in courses in Native American studies can recite facts and information about Indians but cannot necessarily explain where this knowledge originates. Elementary-level students can tell elaborate narratives detailing Indian lifeways and customs; they often draw equally elaborate scenarios in crayon, pen, and pencil. Examples of these drawings are included in the appended resources for Lesson the First.

Despite all of this knowledge, very few students have any detailed knowledge of Indian treaties or any knowledge of dates, facts, or events of Indian history or Michigan Indian history. Many students know of casinos but do not know why Indians can own and operate these businesses. Many students did not know that Indian tribes today have their own governments. However, students know a lot about warfare and warriors. They can draw Indians, tipis, canoes, and arrows. Some students can name Pontiac or Tecumseh but cannot believe that Indians still exist as a culture and people in the state of Michigan.

To test this claim, ask students to describe Indians and Indian lifeways. Ask them what they know about Indians living in the state today. Then, ask them something about early Michigan or U.S. history. For example, name at least one explorer or missionary who visited Michigan before it became a state. Who was the first president of the United States? What tribes comprise the People of the Three Fires of Michigan? Then, for grades 6 to adult, give them the pretest (P-1). This test is designed to make some dramatic points and to gather data while teaching some important facts. Student and teacher answers to the test questions are an important body of information, useful for many of the lessons.

WHAT IS THE PURPOSE OF A PRETEST?

Before delving into the specifics of the lessons, a pretest helps define what students generally know about Indians in U.S. history and/or in contemporary American culture and society. The following test is designed for grades 6 to adult. The purpose is to elicit students' prior knowledge of Indian history and culture and what factors have shaped that knowledge. Answers are provided for the questions on basic knowledge of American history, although these questions should be easy for all students to answer. Answers for questions concerning a basic knowledge of Michigan Indian history are listed on the page following the test.

PROCEDURES FOR TEACHERS

1. Students should work independently for a few minutes to answer the questions. Students should then seek help from other students and the class as a whole. They should find answers to as many questions as possible in twenty minutes.

2. As a class, review the test and identify questions none of the students could answer. Which questions were easy, and which ones were hard? Do students see any correlation between the subject matter of the easy questions and the subject matter of the hard ones?

3. After a brief discussion of the answers to P-1, give P-2 to grades 4 to adult. This test is designed to enable teachers to make some dramatic points and to gather data while teaching some important facts. Student and teacher answers to the test questions are an important body of information, useful for many of the lessons.

ANSWERS TO P-2 AND EXPLORING IDEAS

The answers to the questions are divided between the odd-numbered (general U.S. history) questions and the even-numbered (Indian-specific) questions to give an alternating base of responses.

General U.S. History Answers (Odd Numbers)

1. To name a few, Father Jacques Marquette, Pierre Charlevoix, Louis Jolliet, and Sieur Rene-Robert de La Salle
3. July 4, 1776
5. George Washington
7. 1837
9. George Armstrong Custer
11. Abraham Lincoln
13. CMU Chippewas, Wacousta Warriors, and Okemos Chieftains are a few examples
15. A few are Apache helicopter, Tomahawk missile, and "Geronimo!"

Indian-specific Answers (Even Numbers)

② Chippewas, Ottawas, and Potawatomis

④ Pontiac

⑥ 1836

⑧ Tecumseh

⑩ Company K of the First Michigan Sharpshooters was the most famous Indian unit fighting in the Union army

⑫ 1924 Indian Citizenship Act

⑭ any job can be listed

⑯ 1978

Clarifications: Questions 13 and 15 are informational and fact-finding. Answers to these questions will be useful for many of the lessons that follow. Although question 10 and similar questions ask for specific information, they are designed to surprise: many students will find Indian participation in the Civil War startling. Question 14 is for statistical record keeping: How many students put down some job related to gambling casinos or bingo halls?

The comparison should be obvious between students' base knowledge of U.S. history and their factual knowledge of Michigan Indian history. Children growing up in the U.S. educational system certainly know some U.S. history and core democratic values. Conversely, they may know very little about specific historical events, treaties, or people related to Indian issues. If students know something about Indians, what is the nature of that knowledge? Is what they know based on exposure to images of Indians used to name war weapons or sports teams? Answers to this pretest should provide ample evidence of what students know. The following lessons give some reasonable explanation for why they know what they know.

QUESTIONS FOR THOUGHT AND DISCUSSION

- How aware are we of organized Indian tribes and Indian reservations within the state (some, a little, or a lot)? Do we know their tribal names? If so, write down a few. Do we know where they live? If so, where? Are all Indians in the state members of these tribes (yes, no, unknown)?

- Do we make unsupported assumptions and generalizations about what we do know of Indian people living within our state? If so, do we have evidence of these assumptions in the answers to our pretest that we can list and discuss? How do you know what you know?

- Are we surprised that Michigan Indians would fight in the Union army in the Civil War (1860–65) before they were citizens of Michigan and of the

United States? Why would Indians fight for the United States? Does this change your image of the conventional Indian warrior? Did you know that Michigan Native Americans had a role in the "underground railroad," helping blacks get to Canada during slavery times?

- Why would treaties and religious freedom be important to Indians living in this state? Why would Congress pass a law protecting Indian religious freedom?

APPENDED RESOURCES

Teacher Preparation Handouts

(P-1) How Do We Know What We Know? 15

(P-2) American Indian and U.S. History 16

(P-3) Questions for Thought and Discussion 17

[P-1] HOW DO WE KNOW WHAT WE KNOW?

1. Please describe "Indians" and Indian lifeways.
2. What do you know about Indians living in Michigan today?
3. What do you know about early Michigan or U.S. history? Can you name at least one explorer or missionary who visited Michigan before it became a state?
4. Who was the first president of the United States?
5. What tribes comprise the People of the Three Fires of Michigan?

© PATRICK RUSSELL LEBEAU 2005 / ALL RIGHTS RESERVED

1. Name at least one explorer or missionary who visited Michigan before it became a state.

2. What tribes comprise the Three Fires Confederacy?

3. What day of the year do we celebrate the signing of the Declaration of Independence? What year was this important document signed?

4. After what famous Michigan Indian warrior did the General Motors Corporation name a car division?

5. Who was the first president of the United States?

6. In what year was a treaty signed that ceded most of the land that became the state of Michigan and part of the United States?

7. In what year did Michigan become a state?

8. What was the name of the famous Shawnee leader who fought the Americans in the War of 1812?

9. What was the name of the soldier and leader who fought in the Civil War and who was killed at the Battle of the Little Big Horn fighting Sioux and Cheyenne warriors?

10. Name any Michigan Indians who fought in the Civil War on the Union side, if there are any.

11. Who was the U.S. president during the Civil War?

12. In what year did all Indians in Michigan and the United States become citizens of the United States?

13. Name as many school sports teams (middle schools, high schools, colleges, and universities) as possible that use images of Indians in any way.

14. Today, what jobs do Indians hold in the state of Michigan?

15. Name any military weapons, vehicles, or battle cries with Indian names or connotations.

16. What year did Congress pass the American Indian Religious Freedom Act?

  © **PATRICK RUSSELL LEBEAU 2005 / ALL RIGHTS RESERVED**

[P-3] QUESTIONS FOR THOUGHT AND DISCUSSION

1. How aware are we of organized Indian tribes and Indian reservations within the state (some, a little, or a lot)? Do we know their tribal names? If so, write down a few. Do we know where they live? If so, where? Are all Indians in the state members of these tribes (yes, no, unknown)?

2. Do we make unsupported assumptions and generalizations about what we do know of Indian people living within our state? If so, do we have evidence of these assumptions in the answers to our pretest that we can list and discuss?

3. Are we surprised that Michigan Indians would fight in the Union army in the Civil War (1860–65) before they were citizens of Michigan and the United States? Why would Indians fight for the United States? Does this change your image of the conventional Indian warrior? Did you know that Michigan Native Americans had a role in the "underground railroad," helping blacks get to Canada during slavery times?

4. Why would treaties and religious freedom be important to Indians living in this state? Why would Congress pass a law protecting Indian religious freedom?

© PATRICK RUSSELL LEBEAU 2005 / ALL RIGHTS RESERVED

LESSON
THE
FIRST

Defining our Terms
and Exploring Stereotypes:
Building a Specific Context

MAJOR PREMISE

Stereotypical images of Indians in American culture are influential and have the power to distort an understanding of Native American people and culture.

OBJECTIVES

To demonstrate that:

- Most people do not know many historical facts about Indians.
- Most people can draw an image or picture of an Indian (or Indian theme).
- Most people recognize a tipi drawn with only three lines.
- Images of Indians in American consumer culture are ubiquitous if not overwhelming when we look for them.
- Most people are more likely to encounter stereotypical images of Indians than real, flesh-and-blood Indians.

As a result of these factors, most people will have a distorted view of Indians.

NARRATIVE

The first lesson draws the student's attention to the prolific use of *stereotypical images* of Indians in American consumer culture. Students learn how to identify the components of a stereotypical image. Evidence of these images is easily gathered, sorted, collated, analyzed, and interpreted. After this activity, questions for thought and discussion explore major fallacies inherent in a stereotypical understanding of Indians. For example, of all the images you have gathered, can you identify Chippewas, Ottawas, or Potawatomis or distinguish them from Sioux, Navajos, or Iroquois? How do these images influence our understanding of Indian people? Based on your own experience, are you more likely to encounter an image of an Indian or to meet a real, flesh-and-blood Indian? Further, the point of the lesson is to understand the limitations of general terms such as *Indian* and to learn to use more specific names and terms whenever possible. *Indian* is a powerful term when used in conjunction with the U.S. Constitution but can be demeaning and stereotypical when used as a catchall and inclusive term of reference.

By exploring American Indian stereotypes, students will be able to **identify stereotypical representations** of Indians in American consumer culture: popular literature, children's literature, comic books, role-playing games, television programs and commercials, Hollywood films, and students' imaginations. First, students will discuss names associated with Indians, such as *Native American*. Second, students will discover how stereotypical representations have influenced and continue to influence the understanding of Indians in U.S. history and contemporary society and culture. Third, students will research questions and discuss information found on the World Wide Web and particularly on the Bureau of Indian Affairs Web site to find answers to frequently asked questions.

Can I use the word *Indian?* Yes, using the word *Indian* within very specific contexts is appropriate. *Indian* is a word (a noun) appearing in the U.S. Constitution and serves as the official moniker of recognition of the indigenous peoples of the United States in numerous other governmental and legal documents. Federally recognized Indian tribes such as the Saginaw Chippewa Indian Tribe use this word as part of their legal names. Conversely, *Indian* is a word that also misleads and confuses because of its origins with Columbus. *Indian* refers collectively to all indigenous people in the United States and reduces our understanding to one simple construct. Consequently, most of us are hard-pressed to tell powwow regalia worn by an Ottawa fourth-grade elementary student today from a Hollywood costume worn by an actor in 1955 from the historical garb worn by a Shawnee warrior in 1811. Collectively, and more because of the clothing than the person wearing it, we do "see" and understand them all as "Indian."

Indian and/or *Native American:* *Indian* is used throughout this book, as is the term *Native American*. Most Indians use *Indian* and *Native American* interchangeably, and most Indian organizations, including the National Congress of American Indians and the American Indian Movement, use *Indian* in their titles, as do all Michigan tribes. In addition, many federal laws, such as the

Indian Reorganization Act, and federal agencies, such as the Bureau of Indian Affairs, use *Indian*.

Should I use *Native American*? *Native American* is one way to break down the collective term *Indian* and change its meaning into a reference to flesh-and-blood people whose ancestors lived in Michigan before European Americans visited and settled Michigan land. *Indian* is a convenient term to use when speaking of legal and treaty issues affecting all Native Americans or when investigating stereotypical imagery but is not a good term when speaking of specific cultures and their historical and present-day experiences. A narrowing of focus through a telescoping of terms and names allows for an accurate frame of reference. *Indian* and *Native American* are good general terms to begin an understanding of Michigan's Ottawas, Chippewas, and Potawatomis. But other names, such as Chippewa, Ottawa or Odawa, and Pokagon Band of Potawatomi Indians, produce a more direct reference to the Indians (or Native Americans) of the state of Michigan and an example of one specific group of those Michigan Indians for study and examination.

Names: Michigan's Indian tribes are often referred to by several different names. This book will use the following tribal names: Chippewa (as opposed to Ojibway, Ojibwe, or Ojibwa), Ottawa (as opposed to Odawa), and Potawatomi (as opposed to Udawadamay). As of 2001, Michigan Indians have the following official names: Keneenaw Bay Indian Community, Bay Mills Indian Community, Sault Ste. Marie Band of Chippewa Indians, Hannahville Indian Community, Burt Lake Band of Ottawa and Chippewa Indians, Little Traverse Bay Bands of Odawa Indians, Grand Traverse Band of Ottawa and Chippewa Indians, Little River Band of Ottawa Indians, Saginaw Chippewa Indian Community, Match-e-be-nashshe-wish Band of Pottawatomi, Nottawaseppi Huron Band of Potawatomi Indians, and the Pokagon Band of Potawatomi Indians. *Chippewa, Ottawa*, and *Potawatomi* are also the nouns used on most Michigan Indian treaties. However, at times, due to specific references used and preferences of others, the text may use alternate names or spellings.

Unfortunately, instead of clarifying the legal status of Native Americans in the United States, the use of the noun *Indian* perpetuates stereotypes. *Indian* more often conjures up romantic notions of the noble savage and the collective whole of Native American experience than demonstrates the connection between Indian treaties and the U.S. Constitution or legal matters. *Indian* makes possible the invention of simplistic symbolic constructs that convey the notion of "Indian" in myriad forms. Most people recognize these symbols more often than they recognize a Native American walking down the street.

For example, the **Seven Lines of Stereotypical Iconography** (1.2) shows how simple stereotypical images are easily recognized. The drawing is composed of seven straight lines formed into a tipi and a tomahawk. Why do most people recognize the arrangement of these seven lines as a tipi and a toma-hawk? This recognition confirms that American Indians are a significant part of American culture and underscores the variety of stereotypical perceptions about Indians that exist in contemporary society. The content of such a symbolic device can very easily be assimilated with little conscious thought. Who uses a tipi? Indians. What is the purpose of the tomahawk? To kill? To go to war? These lines are an example of stereotypical Indian iconography in its simplest form.

Most people's imaginations will conjure images of the noble (tipi) and ignoble (tomahawk) Indian, the singular image of the savage warrior. Native Americans, some Americans erroneously believe, were persistently involved in warfare, fighting white Americans and taking enemy scalps. These Indians are presented in the past tense. Images of modern-day Indian people are rarely included as alternatives to these glorious images of the past because modern-day Indians no longer resemble the "great" Indian people of American heritage. Today, Native Americans are more complicated and harder to imagine than a singular stereotypical image. These people cannot easily be drawn with seven straight lines.

Stereotypical imagery is hard to avoid and to ignore, however. A cursory examination of Indian units taught in many elementary schools shows that students draw or otherwise construct artifacts recognized as "Indian": tipis, headbands, canoes, and grocery bag/buckskin outfits. Linking these artifacts to specific Native American people or situating them in a specific time frame is rarely part of the unit's listed goals. Without much effort, these stereotypical artifacts can be used in instruction, but they need a precise and accurate context. The trick is not to avoid or condemn them but to use them with thought and perspective. Tipis, headbands, and canoes can build a specific context of time and place for what teachers and students think they know about Indians who live in tipis, wear headbands, and paddle canoes; that context can change as new knowledge is acquired. Therefore, teachers and students should go out of their way to find and to recognize images that stereotype Native Americans and/or freeze them in the historical past. Artifacts such as feather headdresses obviously influence the way we think about Indians, but we can add to that influence by creating context and perspective by asking and answering questions about the artifacts found in American consumer culture.

An easy first step is to seek out examples of images of Indians in American consumer culture to prove two important points. One is that most of the images found in grocery or toy stores are of warriors or princesses. Second, enough stereotypical examples exist to substantiate the claim that people are more likely to encounter stereotypical images of the American Indian then to meet flesh-and-blood Native American people. Finally, this search for stereotypical imagery shows the prevalence of such imagery in American culture in a way that is hard to ignore. Teachers and students can then understand through the accumulation of images that stereotypes of Indians must influence how Indians are generally perceived.

ACTIVITIES

ACTIVITY A ▶ Definition of "Indian" and Naming

Preparation

1. List possible alternative names for Indian(s). Some alternatives are *Native American, American Indian, Amerindian* (Ethnology), *First Peoples* (Canadian), *Indigenous Americans,* and *Native Peoples.*

General Questions for Thought and Discussion

1. What is the origin of the name *Indian?* Is one name more accurate than another? Is one name more "politically correct" than another? What do you think of names such as *Redskins* or *Braves?* Can these names be offensive? Explain your answer.

2. List all the names of Indian tribes or groups that students know of. Tell them that more than five hundred Indian tribes have official status within the United States today. (*Source:* Frequently Asked Questions on the Bureau of Indian Affairs Web site, *http://www.doi.gov/bureau-indian-affairs.html*)

3. How many different tribes did the class come up with? What tribes do students know? What accounts for their knowledge? Is *tribe* an accurate term? What do you imagine when *tribe* is mentioned? Is *nation* a better term, word, or name? Concerning the definition of *Indian*, which factors are most important to you: legal, biological, political, or social?

4. What do Indians call themselves? This is a very interesting question in terms of time period, geographical location, and the people in question. Names are a product of who is doing the naming. Historians, government officials, and racists will all have different names for Native American people. Share with the students the list of alternative names for the Chippewas (1.1). Research alternative names for the Ottawas and the Potawatomis. Michigan Indian Peoples' names for themselves (i.e., Anishinabe) almost always translate, "the people" or "the original people."

5. What accounts for the differences in names? Why the variety of spellings? How do these names complicate your understanding of the word *Indian* or the phrase *Michigan Indians?*

Preparation

① Have students use a pencil or crayon to create an image of an Indian or an image that can be identified as Indian, but be careful not to suggest any images. Let the students find their own way of representing "Indian" in picture form. Five minutes should be plenty of time. Have the students share their drawings with the class.

② Collect all the student-produced images and create a collage. Display the collage prominently in the classroom for the length of this unit. Share the sample collages in the appended resources with students.

General Questions for Thought and Discussion

① Identify a common theme or an image that is often repeated, such as a headdress or war paint. Why would many of us draw images that are similar or almost alike? How many tipis were drawn? How many war weapons or images that suggest war or warfare were drawn? How many chiefs or Indian men were drawn compared to princesses or Indian maidens? Did anyone draw a picture of Indians in modern times or modern settings? If so, how are they depicted? We have created a set of images. What do they tell us about our understanding of Indians?

② What is a stereotype? Try this sequence: doctor, lawyer, and _____. How do many students fill in the blank? How is this a stereotype? Have students look up the word *stereotype* in several sources. For example, the *American Heritage Dictionary* defines *stereotype* as "a conventional and usually oversimplified conception or belief." Have students work in small groups to look up *stereotype* in a student dictionary. (Social science texts place this word in a human-to-human context. For example, stereotypical reasoning may say that all Indian leaders are chiefs. Chiefs wear war bonnets. Therefore, anyone who wears a war bonnet is an Indian chief.) First, have students share their definitions; then have them compare their pictures to the definitions by sharing the definitions on an overhead projector.

Optional Writing Extension

Have students write a ten- to twelve-sentence paragraph identifying possible sources of information they might have used to produce their images of Indians. Where did they get their ideas about Indians?

Preparation

① Collect several popular magazines that include images of Indians in advertising or professional sports promotion (for example, *People, Sports Illustrated, Better Homes and Gardens, Ladies Home Journal*). You could also use travel brochures from Michigan and other Great Lakes states. Collect enough magazines so that each student or small group of students can have one.

② Have the students search for images of Indians in any form—logos, advertisements, phrases, cartoons, personal ads, photographs, decorative borders, items worn by models or celebrities, or whatever. Have the students cut out these images.

③ Sort the images into groups or themes, such as advertisements for collector plates with Indian themes or Indian collector dolls of various sorts, sports team logos, or profiles of Indian warriors.

④ Create another collage of all these images and display it next to the collage of drawn images.

General Questions for Thought and Discussion

① How do the images found in popular magazines compare to the images drawn by students? Are they similar or different? Are these images possible sources of information for the student-created images? Has anyone in the class ever imagined that so many images of Indians can be so easily found? Why is this so? How do these images resemble or differ from images found in Hollywood movies or television shows?

② Do you see any images that are not stereotypical? Set aside images that are not stereotypical by your best estimation. An example of a non-stereotypical image might be one of an Indian in a contemporary setting or perhaps an Indian driving a car in ordinary clothes. How do these images differ from the stereotypical images? What visual clues lead you to believe that these images are not stereotypical?

Preparation

① Have students explore their households for items such as toys, food containers, or books that contain images of Indians or Indian culture or are somehow associated with Indians in general. If possible, have each student bring at least one item to school.

② Have students present to the class consumer objects from home with Indian motifs. Students should identify the objects and tell where they came from.

General Questions for Thought and Discussion

① Determine, based on what they have learned from activities A–C, whether the item is stereotypical in any way and why. If the object is not apparently stereotypical, the object needs further definition in terms of origin and perhaps tribal affiliation. Some common household items include Big Chief Sugar, Land-o-Lakes Butter, and Indian head bottle openers or novelty coins. Some more precious items such as drums, shields, or beaded jewelry may have been acquired at an Indian powwow or reservation.

ACTIVITY E ▶ Bureau of Indian Affairs Web Site

① The Bureau of Indian Affairs (BIA) Web site is located at *http://www.doi .gov/bia/aitoday/q_and_a.html.*

② This Web site will answer many commonly asked questions about Indians. It does not necessarily provide the only answer for a given question but offers a good starting place for a general understanding of Indian issues. Find the following questions: Who is an Indian? What is an Indian tribe? How does an Indian become a member of a tribe? Do all Indians live on reservations? Are Indians entitled to a free college education? Are Indians U.S. citizens? Did all Indians speak one language? Why are Indians sometimes referred to as *Native Americans?*

③ Instruct each student or team of students to write a list of ten questions they would ask an Indian person and direct them to the BIA Web site to find answers. Have students share their questions and answers with the class.

ACTIVITY F ▶ What Have You Learned?

Writing Extension

Have students express in writing and then in discussion how their knowledge has changed as a result of these activities.

APPENDED RESOURCES

(1.1) Alternative Names for Chippewas 30

(1.2) Seven Lines of Stereotypical Indian Iconography 31

(1.3) Poster Collage 31

(1.4) Poster Collage 32

(1.5) Poster Collage 32

(1.6) Poster Collage with Sports Team Logos 33

(1.7) Detail of Poster Collage 1.6 33

(1.8) Scanner Collage of Found Objects 34

(1.9) Collage of Student, Teacher, and Adult Drawings 35

(1.10) Student Drawing 35

(1.11) Student Drawings 36

(1.12) Student Drawings 36

(1.13) Collage of Sports Team Logos from Michigan Schools 37

(1.14) Questions for Thought and Discussion 38

[1.1] ALTERNATIVE NAMES FOR CHIPPEWAS

The following are alternative names used in a variety of different historical sources and official documents to refer to the Chippewa Indians of Michigan. By 1836, *Chippewa* would emerge as the commonplace spelling and designation. *Chippewa* and *Indian* appear on all Michigan Indian treaties.

Achipoes	**Nation du Sault**
Ahnishinahbaeot-jibway	**Ojebwe**
Anishinaabbeg	**Ojebwa**
Anishinabe	**Ojebway**
Aninishabeg	**Ojibbeway**
Anishinaubae	**Ojibays**
Anishnaubaewuk	**Ojibea**
Anishnaubag	**Ojibwag**
Awishinaubay	**Ojibway**
Bedzaqetcha	**Otchipwe**
Bungees	**Ouchipawah**
Chipeways	**Outhibous**
Chippewaians	**Pillagers**
Chippewas*	**Saulteaux**
Dowaganhas	**Wahkahtowah**
Jibewas	

Ojibwe is also the name of the language spoken by the Indian tribes of Michigan. Within this language, several dialects, including Ojibwe, Potawatomi, and Ottawa, are spoken.

*The name used on all Michigan Indian Treaties

  © PATRICK RUSSELL LEBEAU 2005 / ALL RIGHTS RESERVED

[1.2] SEVEN LINES OF STEREOTYPICAL INDIAN ICONOGRAPHY

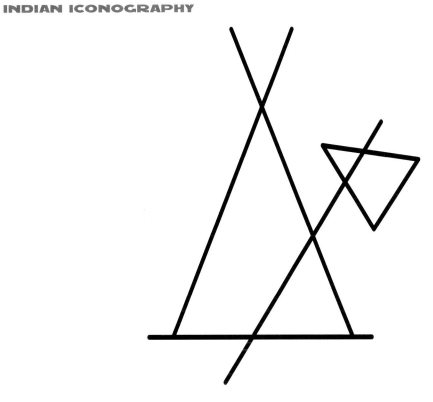

[1.3] POSTER COLLAGE

© PATRICK RUSSELL LEBEAU 2005 / ALL RIGHTS RESERVED

31

  © PATRICK RUSSELL LEBEAU 2005 / ALL RIGHTS RESERVED

[1.6] POSTER COLLAGE WITH SPORTS TEAM LOGOS

[1.7] DETAIL OF POSTER COLLAGE 1.6

© PATRICK RUSSELL LEBEAU 2005 / ALL RIGHTS RESERVED

 © PATRICK RUSSELL LEBEAU 2005 / ALL RIGHTS RESERVED

[1.9] COLLAGE OF STUDENT, TEACHER, AND ADULT DRAWINGS

[1.10] STUDENT DRAWING

© PATRICK RUSSELL LEBEAU 2005 / ALL RIGHTS RESERVED

[1.11] STUDENT DRAWINGS

[1.12] STUDENT DRAWINGS

 © PATRICK RUSSELL LEBEAU 2005 / ALL RIGHTS RESERVED

© PATRICK RUSSELL LEBEAU 2005 / ALL RIGHTS RESERVED

[1.14] QUESTIONS FOR THOUGHT AND DISCUSSION
▶ LESSON THE FIRST

ACTIVITY A ▶ Indian and Naming

1. What is the origin of the name *Indian?* Is one name more accurate than another? Is one name more "politically correct" than another? What do you think of names such as *Redskins* or *Braves?* Can these names be offensive? Explain your answer.

2. List all the names of Indian tribes or groups that you know of.

3. How many different tribes did you come up with? Why are some tribes better known than others? Is *tribe* an accurate term? What do you imagine when *tribe* is mentioned? Is *nation* a better term, word, or name? Concerning the definition of *Indian*, which factors do you feel are most important: legal, biological, political, or social?

4. What do Indians call themselves?

5. What accounts for the differences in names? Why the variety of spellings? How do these names complicate your understanding of the word *Indian* or the phrase *Michigan Indians?*

ACTIVITY B ▶ Drawing Our Own Knowledge

1. Is there a common theme or image that is often repeated? Why would many of us draw images that are similar or almost alike? We have created a set of images. What do they tell us about our understanding of Indians?

2. What is a stereotype? Try this sequence: doctor, lawyer, and _____. How is this a stereotype?

ACTIVITY C ▶ Stereotypes and Consumerism

1. How do the images found in popular magazines compare to the images drawn by you and your fellow students? Are they similar or different? Are these images possible sources of information for the images you created? Did you ever imagine that so many images of Indians could be so easily found? Why is this so? How do these images resemble or differ from images found in Hollywood movies or television shows?

2. Are any of the images not stereotypical? How do these images differ from the stereotypical ones? What visual clues lead you to believe that these images are not stereotypical?

ACTIVITY D ▶ Show-and-Tell of Objects from Home

1. Based on what you have learned from the preceding activities, is each item stereotypical in any way? Why? If the object does not appear to be stereotypical, can you define it further in terms of origin and perhaps tribal affiliation?

 © PATRICK RUSSELL LEBEAU 2005 / ALL RIGHTS RESERVED

LESSON THE SECOND

Challenging the "Great Man" Theory of History

MAJOR PREMISE

Biographies, especially those of Indian warriors, shift the historical focus away from families and communities to heroic deeds, warfare, and killing.

OBJECTIVES

To demonstrate that:

- Biographies of prominent Michigan Indians are more numerous and available than general or specific histories of Michigan Indian families, communities, and larger tribal entities.
- Most Indian biographies focus on men who are warriors and/or leaders, thus perpetuating the notion of the "great man" theory of history.
- In Michigan Indian history, the two most prominent subjects are Tecumseh and Pontiac.
- The focus on warriors and warfare distorts the way students understand Indians in general and Michigan Indians specifically by heightening individuality and individual prowess at the expense of family and community.

NARRATIVE

Lesson the Second examines the biographical treatments of Indian individuals and expands these materials to include Indian families and communities. A biography is an account of a person's life written, composed, or produced by another person. Kings, generals, and statesmen are the most common subjects of biographies.

This lesson advocates the addition to, or expansion of, the "tunnel history" of most biographies about "great" Indians. A need exists to enlarge Indian history to include the communities of both the past and, more importantly, the present. This redirection and broader context is necessary because the popularity of books written on Indian heroes, warriors, and princesses narrows attention to singular acts of valor or individual accomplishment while ignoring the importance of family and community. This lesson shows how biography narrows the vision of Indian history and influences the way we presently think about Indians of the past.

With biographies as a convenient point of departure, students are asked to read about Indian families, communities, and cultures and to search for other sources of information to augment their understanding of the community and culture surrounding the particular subject of the biography. For example, two major U.S. historians, Francis Parkman (*History of the Conspiracy of Pontiac* [1851]) and Howard H. Peckham (*Pontiac and the Indian Uprising of 1763* [1947]), tell a story of warfare and warriors, conflict and soldiers. Parkman and Peckham's narrative histories make the individual, Pontiac, symbolic of Indian identity and character. Contemporary histories, like Gregory Dowd's *A Spirited Resistance: The North American Indian Struggle for Unity, 1745–1815* (1992), offer sensitive portrayals and innovative perspectives but are not as well known as the histories of Parkman and Peckham to teachers and students. In Parkman and Peckham, the Miamis, Ottawas, Chippewas, and Potawatomis become units of armed resistance, combat formations engaged in warfare with colonial America and, later the United States of America rather than cultures and people of other accomplishments. By way of expanding this narrow and limited focus on generalship and combat units, students are asked to read and write on the Chippewa, Ottawa, and Potawatomi cultures and histories from a larger community perspective. Where did Native American people live in 1763, and where do they live today? Do the Ottawas live differently from Chippewas or Miamis? How do these groups differ today from in 1763? Why would an automobile manufacturer name a car division Pontiac?

One answer is that great men of history are often the focus of historical investigation. Most great men—presidents, generals, inventors, scientists, and other heroes—are linked to pivotal turning points or dramatic historical events. For example, George Washington and Abraham Lincoln are well-known figures prominent in the annals of America's history. Numerous accounts of their lives have been written. Most people could explain why these two men are considered important and "great." Could we name dramatic historical events in which these men were involved? Yes: the American Revolution and the American

Civil War. Could we, however, name important women playing prominent roles in America's history in the same eras during which these two men lived? Perhaps we would say Betsy Ross and Sojourner Truth and tell of their good deeds. Mostly, however, we remember more about Washington and Lincoln than Ross and Truth. Why?

Although a very effective way of narrowing history to a manageable form, biographies focus on a single individual and on that individual's deeds and triumphs while limiting our understanding of families and communities. The individual is heightened in importance, and biographies often focus on explaining why individuals are important. Ordinary people are not often the subjects of biography, though more and more biographies of this sort are being written. In K–12 schools, biography's effectiveness at teaching history is generally accepted and with it biography's limitations and influences.

VOCABULARY: THE FALLACY OF THE "GREAT MAN" THEORY OF HISTORY

Fallacy is plausible but invalid reasoning that results when a historian commits a mistake in logic. Good historians make every effort to be impartial and to avoid bias; however, they must make decisions to narrow their subject matter and the length of their investigations. Committing a logical fallacy in history does not mean that the historian is wrong or intended to mislead. To the contrary, most historians welcome critical analysis of their work. All historians are fallible and can be challenged by critical analysis.

In the teaching of Native American history, the fallacy inherent in the "great man" theory of history is the way these biographies influence and narrow our thinking on certain subjects, such as Indian warriors. For example, consider the numerous popular biographies of Pontiac and Tecumseh in print today. By 1999, more than thirty biographies of these two men had been published. These works eclipse the relatively few histories on the Native American People of Michigan, let alone on individual tribes or contemporary issues. Combine this popular interest in "great" Indian warriors with the many stereotypical representations of Indians present in American culture (see Lesson the First), and a distorted and limited view of Native Americans is not hard to imagine.

SHORT BIOGRAPHIES OF PONTIAC AND TECUMSEH

Pontiac (ca. 1720–1769), an Ottawa, is known as the leader of the Indian uprising of 1763 in which Michigan's Indians besieged and stormed several British Forts in the Old Northwest, including Fort Detroit and Fort Michilimackinac.

In 1763, Ottawa warriors took Fort Michilimackinac by playing a lacrosse game at the fort's gate, thereby inducing defenders to let their guard down. Pontiac was involved in the siege of Fort Detroit, which the British successfully defended.

Tecumseh (1768–1813), a Shawnee, is known as the leader of a 1805–1813 movement to unite all the tribes west of U.S. borders to stop further U.S. expansion into Indian territories. He allied himself with the British during the War of 1812. He was killed on October 5, 1813, at the Battle of Moraviantown (near the River Thames) in Ontario, Canada.

Because of their role as popular biographical subjects, Pontiac and Tecumseh are remembered as warriors and statesmen rather than as fathers, husbands, or members of a greater Native American community. The titles of biographies of Pontiac and Tecumseh direct readers' attention to this warrior guise and comparisons to Western definitions of leadership steer readers to ideas of kings, generals, and defenders. Examples of parts of titles or subtitles of biographies that illustrate this point include "Indian General and Statesman," "King of the Great Lakes," "The Death of," "The Conspiracy of," "Shawnee War Chief," "The Defenders," "Fight for the Old North West," "Ottawa Rebel," "Forest Warrior," and "Indian Uprising."

If we shift focus to lesser-known Native American individuals such as Michigan's Leopold Pokagon (St. Joseph River Potawatomi) and Andrew J. Blackbird (Little Traverse Ottawa), we must remain wary of standard definitions of leadership or the importance of "great men" in Western culture. This approach does not tell the whole story of Michigan's Indians or their ability to adapt and live as vibrant and viable cultural entities in Michigan today.

SHORT BIOGRAPHIES OF ANDREW BLACKBIRD AND LEOPOLD POKAGON

In 1887, Andrew Blackbird wrote and published a book, *History of the Ottawa and Chippewa Indians of Michigan,* that offered a grammar of their language and a personal and family history of the author. He wanted to record the ancient legends and traditions of his people, the Ottawas and Chippewas who lived (and live) on the land between Little Traverse Bay and the Straits of Mackinac. More importantly, he recorded his people's and his own efforts to continue as a viable culture and people during a transitional period, 1820–90.

Leopold Pokagon was born around 1776 and died on July 18, 1841. He was born a Chippewa but was adopted as a child by a Potawatomi, Topenibe. Historian James Clifton claims that the name "Pokagon means something like Mr. Rib." Pokagon's clan was Sakekwinik, River's Mouth, and his people's homeland was the St. Joseph River Valley area. As a Potawatomi leader, Pokagon was determined that his people remain a viable and thriving community on or near their traditional homelands.

Men such as Blackbird and Pokagon are generally called "chiefs" and are often erroneously believed to be more like kings than men who represent the concerns of Indian families and communities. But like Pontiac and Tecumseh, Blackbird and Pokagon represented the concerns and sentiments of their families and communities in times of crisis and change. Unlike Pontiac and Tecumseh, however, Blackbird and Pokagon were not the "typical" warriors engaged in armed resistance favored by most biographers of Indian subjects; thus, Blackbird and Pokagon have not become examples of historians illustrating trends and motivations of larger groups and communities. Despite their relative obscurity in the historical record (not many adults would know their names), Pokagon and Blackbird emerge as leaders because they were present at treaty negotiations and signings and because they argued for treaty rights in courts and other official proceedings. They were in position to help because their people trusted them. In true democratic fashion, they represented and spoke for their families and communities. They were not absolute monarchs; they were not despots.

After Michigan's Native Americans were militarily defeated and no longer a military threat, the popular focus of U.S. history and biography moves westward; Michigan's nonmilitary Native American leaders, including Pokagon and Blackbird, would not be popular biographical subjects. In the mid- to late-1800s, they were not as interesting as Blackhawk, Red Cloud, Sitting Bull, Chief Joseph, and Geronimo. Pokagon and Blackbird's contributions to cultural survival and their fight for the rights, land, and money promised in treaties are just as important as fighting back in a military way, even if such actions are less romantic and "action packed." Students need to know this overlooked history. Native Americans needed leaders to assure that treaties were honored, that people had a place to live, and that they had a means to make a living.

Michigan's Indians live today as viable cultural/political entities because their ancestors (Pokagon and Blackbird are representative examples) developed sophisticated tactics for adapting in the 1800s while holding onto cultural values and staying close to their home territories. No longer completely self-sufficient and independent by 1830, Michigan's Native Americans had to sign treaties, cede most of their communal land base, and accept a place in U.S.-European culture, society, and economy. In the period 1836–55, the U.S. government tried to force its ideas of "civilization" on the Michigan Indians by threatening to move them west of the Mississippi River. With the signing of the 1855 Michigan Indian Treaties, most of the egregious forms of Indian Removal were revoked, but many Michigan Indians were still removed to the Indian territories or fled to Canada. In their own way, and for the purpose of remaining in Michigan, these Native Americans became "civilized," and by so doing, they survived.

If we examine the biographies of Pokagon and Blackbird rather than the traditional "warriors and warfare" biographies of Pontiac and Tecumseh, we will learn more about Native American *people*, *families*, and *communities*. The historical investigation, then, can go beyond the focus of glorious individuals to include ordinary Native Americans and their concerns. Using biography as a starting point and adding more about the lives of Native Americans in the 1880s, we can learn more about how Michigan's Native American people survived adversity and emerged today as families, tribes, and governments.

One example is the St. Joseph River Potawatomis and Pokagon. They persisted as a viable community despite decades of warfare, the ceding or surrendering of their land through treaties, the meager annuity goods and cash payments, and U.S. Indian policy, such as the civilization policy and Indian removal. A critical examination of the tactics designed and used by these Potawatomis between 1825 and 1842 reveals Native Americans who were more complex than the stereotypical and popular image of them found in traditional U.S. history texts. "Indian survival and assimilation" simplifies the real power of these historical Potawatomis to adapt to changing circumstances while remaining recognizable as Potawatomi.

In another example, Blackbird wrote his *History of the Ottawa and Chippewa Indians of Michigan* (1887), which differs in many ways from the kind of history we are used to reading. Like Pokagon, Blackbird was born, raised, and died in Michigan. He lived mostly in and around Harbor Springs during the mid- to late 1800s. His book includes family and personal history as well as a general history of his people. He presents cultural beliefs and practices alongside the political and economic concerns of Ottawas and Chippewas. He recounts mythological stories of origin and migration. He even adds a lamentation written in the style of the romantic poets of the time. His book offers students a unique opportunity for investigation and analysis of Indians of Michigan in a historical setting. Rather than a detached and distant view from the outside, students can learn about Indian character and lifeways from a directed reading of a book written by someone within one of the many Native American communities located in Michigan's not-so-distant past.

PART 1 ▶ WARRIORS AND WARS: PONTIAC AND TECUMSEH

Introduction

The focus on warriors and wars does a disservice to living Native Americans. The romantic ideal created by historians and writers of historical fiction is hard to live up to. In addition, focusing too much on historical characters freezes, for most students, Native American people in the past tense and diminishes the relevance of Native Americans living in the present. The narrowing of the subject to individuals equally ignores the family and community. Warriors are killed in acts of combat or fade away as broken or defeated defenders of Indian land. Families and communities survive and thrive but in the coming years are not seen as a glorious people. Rather, compared to the honorable warrior, they are often viewed as degenerate descendants of the "great men" of Indian history who continue to exist as a result of the benevolence of their vanquishers. Therefore, treaties, treaty rights, adaptation, and accommodation are subjects and themes not often explored because they pale in comparison to the mighty chiefs and rebel warriors of America's past and because this interpretation is based on the "great men" of Indian history being defeated or dying. Great Indian men continue to be taught and honored in Michigan classrooms despite that the "great man" theory of history is considered obsolete by all contemporary historians.

Objectives

- To show how a historian's selection of topic and information provided in a biography limits what can be learned and understood.
- To show the power of words and images to influence thinking.
- To demonstrate that history books about Indians, especially ones meant for school-age children, are mostly biographies.
- To provide evidence that many of these biographies focus on warriors and warfare to the exclusion of contemporary issues or people, especially in Michigan.
- To show that students need to research and expand their understanding of Indians beyond the dominant influences created by biographies of singular Indian warriors.

Preparation

1. In class discussion, name and list five American revolutionary leaders or signers of the Declaration of Independence. Name and list five prominent women, African Americans, Native Americans, or members of any other group active in the same era, 1776–1800.

2. Have students read the "Selected Titles of Biographies of Pontiac and Tecumseh" (2.2). Have them study the words carefully.

3. Have students find and list all keywords that denote the idea of leadership. For example, "Mighty Chief" is a possible combination.

4. Have students find definitions of the identified keywords in a standard American dictionary. Some keywords are as follows: *chief, warrior, leader, nation, general,* and *statesman.*

5. Have students list other words that may have emotional power or meaning —for example, *mighty, vision, conspiracy, conquest,* and *rebel.*

6. Have students find and list definitions of *leadership* in Western civilization. Look for examples of statesmen, generals, and captains of industry in American culture and history. How is George Washington a leader?

Questions for Thought and Discussion

1. What is leadership? What are the characteristics of leadership?

2. How do the titles of these books influence our thinking? What emotions, if any, do they evoke? What story do they tell in and of themselves?

3. Think of the titles as a whole. What is the major theme that connects them all? Why are there so many similarities?

4. Do you detect any definition of *leadership* in the group? If so, what words are used to indicate "leader"?

5. How would you define *conspiracy, massacre, rebel,* and *uprising,* and what do these words say about the authors' points of view? What do these words suggest about the character of the Indians in question? [Show students the collages of Pontiac and Tecumseh (2.3 and 2.4). Can these words be used to describe these pictures?]

Preparation

1. Have students look for biographies of famous Indian warriors in your library. You should first look for biographies of Pontiac and Tecumseh, but

any famous warrior will do. For comparative purposes, look for biographies of Native American non-warriors, like Sacajawea or Maria Tallchief.

② Check out as many of these books as possible and bring them to your classroom.

③ Share the "Collage of Images of Book Covers of Biographies of Pontiac and Tecumseh" and "Collage of Images of Pontiac and Tecumseh" (2.3 and 2.4).

④ Look through the books that have been checked out for any illustrations, drawings, lithographs, or paintings of Indian warriors.

Questions for Thought and Discussion

① What general theme emerges as you look at the images of Pontiac, Tecumseh, and other Indian warriors?

② Describe the demeanors, stances, and faces of Pontiac and Tecumseh. What do you imagine they are thinking?

③ What kind of clothes are they wearing? What do these clothes say about their occupation or preoccupation?

④ Can you find examples of Western influences such as clothing or other material objects? What does the presence of these Western influences mean?

⑤ Did you find women or children depicted in any of the images you examined? What images dominate, and how do they contribute to the book's intent and focus?

⑥ How are warriors drawn (depicted)? What similarities exist? Differences? Can you tell an Ottawa warrior from a Shawnee? How do Woodland Indian warriors differ from Sioux Indian warriors? How are they alike?

⑦ Why would an automobile manufacturer name a car division Pontiac? Are there other automobiles named after Indian warriors, Indian warrior themes, or Indian subject matter in general?

Activity C ▶ Expanding the Native American World beyond Warriors and Warfare

Preparation

① This activity uses research and investigation, so results may vary depending on time constraints, library resources, and resources found outside the school or classroom.

② First, have students look for books on the Ottawas, Chippewas, and Potawatomis. Look for books on culture, artistic expression, and contemporary issues. Try not to rely on Native American students (if any) in your classroom to supply information or as resource persons unless they volunteer information.

③ Photocopy "Culturally Relevant History Books for Student Investigation" (2.5) and share it with students. This list can be used by itself for a simpler variation of the activity. The titles on this list suggest a different historical focus than the biographies of warriors or other stereotypical works. You can establish a very effective contrast of subject matters just by comparing "Selected Titles of Biographies of Pontiac and Tecumseh" (2.2) to the "Culturally Relevant History Books" (2.5). Photocopy-ready "Questions for Thought and Discussion" (2.14) for each activity are also appended. Many of these questions are applicable to more than one activity.

Questions for Thought and Discussion

① Where did Indian people live in 1763 and 1812, and where do they live today?

② Do the Ottawas live differently than Chippewas or Potawatomis?

③ How do they differ today from 1763 and 1812? How are they alike? Can you answer these questions? Why or why not?

④ How many books did you find on the Indian People of Michigan? How many books did you find about Indian warriors or leaders? What accounts for the difference, if any, in the number?

⑤ Look at the titles listed in the "Selected Titles of Biographies of Pontiac and Tecumseh" (2.2) and the "Culturally Relevant History Books for Student Investigation" (2.5). How do they differ? What does the second list convey as the focus and subjects of the books? How do the words in the titles differ?

PART 2 ▶ LEOPOLD POKAGON AND ANDREW BLACKBIRD IN THE 1800S

Introduction

This section is meant as a stand-alone set of defined objectives and thinking questions to examine any Native American biography. The goal is to look for facts and information about how Native Americans persevered through dramatic times and are a more complex people than the simplicity of stereotypes of warriors and wars would have us believe. For full citations to the sources mentioned in the activities, see Selected Instructional/Research Resources for Teachers. The summaries found in the appended resources (2.7 and 2.8) and your own library resources (biographies of any Native American will do) can be critically examined using the questions and methods presented in this section. Students are encouraged to think about Native Americans' motivations and actions for survival.

We want to move students away from the idea of Native Americans as victims or agents merely reacting to events over which they had no control. Native Americans certainly understood that survival meant adaptation and change. They understood that diplomacy and cooperative effort would enable them to control their destinies. They also knew that they did not have to surrender cultural values or integrity to find a meaningful life in contemporary America. The summaries of the lives of Pokagon and Blackbird (2.7 and 2.8), the background information handout (2.1), and the cover of the *History of the Ottawa* (2.9) found in the appended resources provide enough detail for the specific purpose of this lesson.

Objectives

- To explore the civilization policy and Indian removal.
- To compare and contrast Western notions of leadership to Potawatomi, Chippewa, and Ottawa notions of leadership.
- To explore the tactics employed by Pokagon and his colleagues that enabled them to remain a cohesive community, both culturally and politically, to stay close to their homeland, to resist removal, and to persist as a people still called Potawatomis.
- To examine the role of Christianity in Potawatomi culture and society.
- To explore Michigan Indians' perspectives and understandings of the 1836 Treaty of Washington and the 1855 Treaties of Detroit.
- To explore the importance of education for the Indian people of Michigan.
- To explore how Pokagon and Blackbird challenge and contradict stereotypical representations of their people.
- To explore how Pokagon and Blackbird's stories differ from textbook history and to explore the significance of those differences.

Activity A ▶ Treaties and Removal

Questions for Thought and Discussion

① How did Pokagon resist removal? How were he and his people able to stay in the state of Michigan? What strategies did he develop to remain in the state? What did the Potawatomis have to do to stay?

② Why was it so important for Pokagon and his people to remain near and around their homeland? (Think of practical and emotional reasons why you might want to stay close to your home.)

③ How can biographers counter romantic fantasies of "Great Chief" or "Great Friend of the White Man" in describing Pokagon's actions? Why? How can biographers convey to their readers the idea of ordinary Indians contributing to the welfare of their people? How can biographers create an impression of family/community? How is Pokagon less "extraordinary" than an Indian warrior such as Pontiac?

④ According to Blackbird, did U.S. government officials honor their country's treaty obligations?

⑤ What is the purpose of exchanging land for money, farming equipment, and an education in the "manners and customs of the white man?"

⑥ From the perspective of the United States, what is the definition of a "civilized" Indian?

⑦ Is Blackbird "civilized"? Is Pokagon "civilized"?

⑧ Can a Native American be "civilized" and still retain "Indian" ways? Explain. What are "Indian" ways as you have encountered them in the readings? Give specific examples.

⑨ How does Blackbird show or share his Ottawa identity with his readers?

⑩ How did Michigan Native Americans avoid removal?

Activity B ▶ The Importance of a White Man's Education to Leopold Pokagon and Andrew Blackbird

Questions for Thought and Discussion

① What would motivate a Native American to get an education? (Briefly define "an education.")

② List the advantages of an education for a Native American.

③ Why would someone not want Indians to be educated?

④ Why is citizenship so important to Blackbird?

Activity C ▶ How Do Pokagon and Blackbird Counter Stereotypical Representations of Indian People?

Questions for Thought and Discussion

① Explain your understanding of Native Americans living in Michigan in the 1800s.

② After reading about Pokagon and Blackbird, do you have a different view and understanding of Indians who lived in Michigan from 1830 to 1890? Explain these differences. How do Pokagon's and Blackbird's histories change your view of Native Americans who lived in Michigan from 1830 to 1890?

③ What do the twenty-one precepts listed at the end of Blackbird's history tell you about the character of a traditional Ottawa person?

④ Write a summary of what you have learned from Pokagon and Blackbird about Indian life from 1830 to 1890.

Activity D ▶ Leadership

Questions for Thought and Discussion

① Historian James Clifton presents an alternative analysis of Michigan Indian leadership. Pokagon is not a typical leader as defined by most biographers and historians. What is the common definition of a leader? Why is a leader heroic? How does Pokagon differ from this ideal? Would Pokagon enjoy being singled out as special? How does he differ from your understanding of Pontiac or Tecumseh as leaders?

② Define an "Indian" leader. What is the purpose of leadership in Indian communities in the 1880s? Is being a leader for self-gratification a part of the Indian definition? If so, give some examples from the readings. If not, give some examples of how, as Clifton writes, leaders, or *Wkameks*, were reminded daily that "they were no more than first among equals." Give some examples of how this statement applies to Pokagon. Think of well-known non–Native American leaders. Does "first among equals" apply to them?

③ Why does Clifton avoid the term *hero?* Why is *hero* not applicable to Pokagon or Blackbird? Does the word *hero* apply to Pontiac and Tecumseh? How can this word influence or perhaps distort our thinking?

④ Is the Western understanding of leadership (generals, kings, and statesmen) a fair way of describing Native American individuals? How? How is it not fair? Write a new definition that incorporates both Western and Native American perspectives.

Activity E ▶ Christianity

Preparation

① Copy Blackbird's "The Twenty-one Precepts of the Ottawa and Chippewa" (2.10) and distribute to students or student groups. Have them read the precepts.

Questions for Thought and Discussion

1. Does or did conversion to Christianity bestow any political or economic advantage to Native American people? If so, explain the details.

2. Why did Pokagon and the Potawatomis decide not to be Baptists any longer and to convert to Catholicism?

3. Chapter 14 of Blackbird's *History of the Ottawa* has the "The Twenty-one Precepts of the Ottawa and Chippewa" in English followed by the "Ten Commandments," "The Creed," and the "Lord's Prayer" in Ottawa. Are you, as a careful reader, meant to learn something from the twenty-one precepts? What kind of life (or way of life) do these precepts suggest that a person should live? Explain your answer.

4. How are the Ottawa-Chippewa precepts listed in Blackbird's history comparable to the Bible's Ten Commandments? Can a Native American be Christian and still stay true to many aspects of traditional Native American culture? Does one way of life have to exclude the other?

PART 3 ▶ HISTORICAL JUXTAPOSITIONS: THREE FIRES PEOPLE IN THE CIVIL WAR

Introduction

After the Civil War, some Native Americans living in Michigan earned citizenship by meeting the requirements of "civilization" prescribed by the federal and state governments. In 1924, the Indian Citizenship Act granted all Native Americans citizenship. During the Civil War, more than a hundred Ottawas, Chippewas, and Potawatomis served in the Union army to show their loyalty to their state and nation and to prove that they met the requirements of "civilization." They did not want more of their land to be taken away; they did not want to be removed from their homesteads or be accused of disloyalty or rebellious activities.

Objectives

For students, Michigan Native Americans Three Fires People serving as soldiers in the Union army may come as a surprise. That is the point. The idea of the stereotypical Indian warrior is put into question and perhaps smashed by the notion of Native Americans dressed in Union blue uniforms. From the Civil War to the Iraq War, Native Americans residing in the state have served in

America's wars with honor and distinction. These warriors are often overlooked or ignored in the face of the attention on the warriors of savage distinction found in the books explored earlier in this lesson.

Preparation

① Give students the handouts on "Company K of the First Michigan Sharpshooters" (2.11), the daguerreotype of Payson Wolfe (2.12), and the "Narrative Explanation of the Daguerreotype of Payson Wolfe" (2.13).

② Discuss the idea of historical juxtapositions by pointing out the unexpected and alien idea of Indians participating in the American Civil War.

③ Compare the image of Payson Wolfe with images of Pontiac, Tecumseh, and other warriors found in standard history textbooks.

④ Share the fact that Native Americans have served in many wars on the side of the United States. My grandfather, for example, served as a doughboy (a U.S. foot soldier) in World War I before he was a U.S. citizen.

Questions for Thought and Discussion

① Is it hard to imagine Michigan Native Americans serving as soldiers in the Union army in the American Civil War? Why or why not?

② What would motivate Native Americans to serve in a military that at times fought wars against the Three Fires people and would fight wars with Indian people west of the Mississippi between 1865 and 1900?

③ How does this information change your understanding of the Indian warrior depicted in many history books?

④ How does the image of Payson Wolfe influence your thinking about stereotypical images of Indian warriors?

⑤ What evidence can you draw on to demonstrate that Payson Wolfe is still an Odawa? How has he adapted to changing times? What evidence can you find in the handouts that Payson Wolfe is a loyal resident of the state of Michigan and of the Union? Explain your answer.

⑥ Are these Michigan Union soldiers not "Indian" any more because they have served? What does their service say about change and adaptation to dramatic events? Are they any less heroic or less brave for having served?

APPENDED RESOURCES

(2.1) Background Information 57

Part 1: Warriors and Wars: Pontiac and Tecumseh

(2.2) Selected Titles of Biographies of Pontiac and Tecumseh 58

(2.3) Collage of Tecumseh Book Covers 59

(2.4) Collage of Images of Tecumseh and Pontiac 60

(2.5) Culturally Relevant History Books for Student Investigation 61

Part 2: Leopold Pokagon and Andrew Blackbird in the 1800s

(2.6a–b) Pretest for Part 2 62

(2.7) Summary of Leopold Pokagon's Life 64

(2.8) Summary of Andrew Blackbird's Life 65

(2.9) Cover of Blackbird's *History* 65

(2.10) Blackbird's "The Twenty-one Precepts of the Ottawa and Chippewa" . 66

Part 3: Historical Juxtapositions: Michigan Native Americans in the Civil War

(2.11) Company K of the First Michigan Sharpshooters, Union Army,
      American Civil War, 1863–1865 68

(2.12) Narrative Explanation of Daguerreotype of Payson Wolfe,
      Grand River Band Odawa and Member of Company K,
      First Michigan Sharpshooters 69

(2.13) Glass Plate Daguerreotype of Payson Wolfe 69

(2.14) Questions for Thought and Discussion 70

① Treaties are solemn agreements between two sovereign nations and are upheld by the U.S. Constitution. Treaties are also contracts, and any exchanges or promises that are specified within them must be carried out.

② The 1795 Treaty of Greenville, the 1807 Treaty of Detroit, the 1815 Treaty of Spring Wells, the 1819 Treaty of Saginaw, the 1821 Treaty of Chicago, the 1836 Treaty of Washington, the 1842 Treaty of LaPointe conveyed the lands that would become the state of Michigan to the United States of America.

③ In return for all this land, Michigan Indians would get annuities (money), agricultural equipment, experts to help them to learn skills and professions of the average American citizen, and schools (or schooling) to teach Indian children reading, writing, and arithmetic.

④ The 1830 Indian Removal Act specified that those Indians who did not become Christian, landowners, gainfully employed, and taxpayers were not "civilized" and, therefore, could be moved to lands west of the Mississippi.

⑤ Indian leaders act for their people. Indians believed that land should be owned collectively. The federal government and the state of Michigan pressured Indians to become individual landowners, in the 1855 treaties allotting separate parcels.

⑥ Trust land is land held by the federal government for Indian people. This land is "reserved" for their specific use.

⑦ Except for the Detroit area, Michigan was still "Indian country" in 1830. The opening of the Erie Canal flooded Southern Michigan, placing pressure for removing the Potawatomi. Indians living north of Grand Rapids retained their traditional lifestyle until about 1870. They changed from hunting to lumbering in many areas. Lumbering continued well into the 20th century. Land pressure in northern Michigan and the Upper Peninsula was not significant until the 1940s.

© PATRICK RUSSELL LEBEAU 2005 / ALL RIGHTS RESERVED

[2.2] SELECTED TITLES OF BIOGRAPHIES OF PONTIAC AND TECUMSEH

Pontiac

The Conspiracy of Pontiac and the Indian War after the Conquest of Canada:
    To the Massacre at Michilimackinac, by Francis Parkman
Forest Warrior: The Story of Pontiac, by Jill Wheeler
Pontiac, Chief of the Ottawas, by Jane Fleischer
Pontiac, Indian General and Statesman, by Matthew G. Grant
Pontiac and the Indian Uprising, by Howard H. Peckham
Pontiac, King of the Great Lakes, by C. Hollmann
Pontiac: Mighty Ottawa Chief, by Virginia Frances Voight
Pontiac, by Celia Bland
Pontiac: Ottawa Rebel, by Celia Bland and W. David Baird
A Spirited Resistance: The North American Indian Struggle for Unity, 1745–1815,
    by Gregory Dowd

Tecumseh

The Death of Tecumseh, by Pierre Berton
The Defenders: Osceola, Tecumseh, and Cochise, by Ann McGovern
God Gave Us This Country: Tekamthi and the First American Civil War,
    by Bil Gilbert
Lives of Famous Indian Chiefs, by Norman B. Wood
Panther in the Sky, by James A. Thorn (novel based on the life of Tecumseh)
Patriot Chiefs, by Alvin Josephy
A Sorrow in Our Heart: The Life of Tecumseh, by Allan W. Eckert
Tecumseh: A Chronicle of the Last Great Leader of His People, by Ethel T. Raymond
Tecumseh and the Dream of an American Indian Nation, by Russell Shorto
Tecumseh's Last Stand, by John Sugden
Tecumseh, Leader, by D. L. Brichfield
Tecumseh and the Quest for Indian Leadership, by R. David Edmunds
Tecumseh: Shawnee Rebel, by Robert Cwiklik
Tecumseh: Shawnee War Chief, by Jane Fleischer
Tecumseh, the Story of the Shawnee Chief, by Luella B. Creighton (children's book)
Tecumseh: Vision of Glory, by Glen Tucker
"Tecumseh; or, The Warrior of the West," by John Richardson (poem)
These Lands Are Ours: Tecumseh's Fight for the Old Northwest, by Kate Connell

 © PATRICK RUSSELL LEBEAU 2005 / ALL RIGHTS RESERVED

© PATRICK RUSSELL LEBEAU 2005 / ALL RIGHTS RESERVED

 © PATRICK RUSSELL LEBEAU 2005 / ALL RIGHTS RESERVED

Benton-Banai, Edward. *The Mishomis Book: The Voice of the Ojibway.* Michigan Indian Press, 1981.

Blackbird, Andrew. *History of Ottawa and Chippewa Indians of Michigan: A Grammar of Their Language and Personal and Family History of the Author.* 1887; reprint, Petoskey, Mich.: Little Traverse Regional Historical Society, 1967.

Bleeker, Sonia. *The Chippewa Indians: Rice Gatherers of the Great Lakes.* New York: William Morrow, 1955.

Bussey, M. T., comp., with legends by Simon Otto. *Aube Na Bing: A Pictorial History of Michigan Indians, 1865–1988.* Grand Rapids: Michigan Indian Press, 1989.

Clifton, James. *The Pokagons, 1683–1983: Catholic Potawatomi Indians of the St. Joseph River Valley.* New York: University Press of America, 1984.

Clifton, James. *The Potawatomi.* New York: Chelsea House, 1987.

Densmore, Frances. *The Chippewa Customs.* Minneapolis: Ross and Haines, 1970.

Greene, Jacqueline D. *The Chippewa.* New York: Franklin Watts, 1993.

Haslam, Andrew, and Alexandra Parsons. *Make It Work: North American Indians.* New York: Thomson Learning, 1995.

Hofsinde, Robert. *Indians at Home.* New York: William Morrow, 1964.

Johnston, Basil. *Ojibway Ceremonies.* Toronto: McClelland and Stewart, 1982.

Johnston, Basil. *Ojibway Heritage.* Toronto: McClelland and Stewart, 1976.

King, Sandra. *Shannon: An Ojibway Dancer.* Minneapolis: Lerner Publications, 1993.

Lucas, Eileen. *The Ojibwas.* Brookfield, Conn.: Millbrook Press, 1994.

McClurken, James M. *Gah-Baeh-Jhagwah-Buk = The Way It Happened: A Visual Culture History of the Little Traverse Bay Bands of Odawa.* East Lansing: Michigan State University Museum, 1991.

Tanner, Helen Hornbeck, ed. *The Atlas of Great Lakes Indians.* Norman and London: The University of Oklahoma Press, 1987.Wub-e-ke-niew. *We Have the Right to Exist: A Translation of Aboriginal Indigenous Thought: The First Book Ever Published from an Ahnishinahb Ojibway Perspective.* New York: Black Thistle Press, 1995.

© PATRICK RUSSELL LEBEAU 2005 / ALL RIGHTS RESERVED

Instructions

Ask students to prepare answers to the following questions. Have students explain their *yes* or *no* answers. The answers can be shared after student answers are aired and discussed.

1. Do Indians live in Michigan today? If so, where do they live? How do they live? Why do you think Indians still survive as a recognizable people?

2. Did Indians living in Michigan during the period 1830–90 know how to read or write in the English language?

   Pokagon's book proves that the answer is yes. Show the cover of the book to the class (2.9).

3. Could these same Indians vote during this time?

   In 1850, the State of Michigan revised its constitution and granted state citizenship to "civilized" Native peoples of Michigan. Blackbird writes on p. 98 of his book, "By the Kindness of the people of the State of Michigan, they [Indians] were adopted as citizens and made equal in rights with their white neighbors. Their voice was to be recognized in the ballot box in every election." On p. 65, Blackbird shares his first voting experience. However, votes by Indians were often rescinded when Indians voted contrary to the wishes of the Indian agent, a non-Indian appointee of the federal government.

4. In the mid- to late-1880s, could Indians attend school or hold regular jobs in cities, towns, or rural areas?

   Blackbird went to Ypsilanti Normal School. He held a variety of jobs from farmhand to postmaster of Little Traverse (now Harbor Springs).

 © PATRICK RUSSELL LEBEAU 2005 / ALL RIGHTS RESERVED

[2.6b] PRETEST FOR PART 2

1. Do Indians live in Michigan today? If so, where do they live? How do they live? Why do you think Indians still survive as a recognizable people?

2. Did Indians living in Michigan during the period 1830–90 know how to read or write in the English language?

3. Could these same Indians vote during this time?

4. In the mid- to late-1880s, could Indians attend school or hold regular jobs in cities, towns, or rural areas?

© PATRICK RUSSELL LEBEAU 2005 / ALL RIGHTS RESERVED

[2.7] SUMMARY OF LEOPOLD POKAGON'S LIFE

According to the historian James Clifton, Native American leaders such as Leopold Pokagon were equals within Potawatomi villages and society, not commanding figures with absolute power and control. Clifton writes, "The position of *Wkama*, their word for leader, was neither hereditary nor loaded with powers and prerogatives" (18). *King, noble,* or *general* is not the proper noun to describe a "leader" in Potawatomi society. Power and wealth were dispersed in the culture, not concentrated or hoarded. Potawatomi leaders emerged as leaders because they were selected as the best spokesmen for the village or group as a whole. They had the ability to negotiate with the outside world on behalf of all members of their communities. With this designated official speaker status, they represented the group to non-Potawatomis, including missionaries, government agents and officials, and U.S. Army officers.

Leopold Pokagon was born around 1776 and died on July 18, 1841. He was born a Chippewa but was adopted as a child by a Potawatomi, Topenibe. Clifton claims that the name "Pokagon means something like Mr. Rib" (18). Pokagon's clan was Sakekwinik, River's Mouth, and his people's homeland was the St. Joseph River Valley area. As a Potawatomi leader, Pokagon was determined that his people would remain a viable and thriving community on or near their traditional homelands.

Pokagon negotiated favorable terms in land cession treaties and formed alliances with Catholic missionaries. His people invested treaty annuities (money) by purchasing land. They went to grammar school and learned mathematics, reading, and writing. They learned to farm their land. By 1838, according to Clifton, "they were treaty-abiding, farming, Christian, land-owning, tax-paying, sedentary Potawatomi Indian citizens of the new State of Michigan." Hence, with Pokagon's leadership, they avoided removal from the state and cultural and social annihilation by adapting to dramatically new situations.

Source: James A. Clifton, "Transformative Leadership on the St. Joseph River Frontier," *Michigan History* (September–October 1985): 17–23.

 © PATRICK RUSSELL LEBEAU 2005 / ALL RIGHTS RESERVED

In 1887, Andrew Blackbird wrote and published a book, *History of the Ottawa and Chippewa Indians of Michigan*, a grammar of their language and a personal and family history of the author. He wanted to record the ancient legends and traditions of his people, the Ottawas and Chippewas who lived (and live) on the land between Little Traverse Bay and the Straits of Mackinac. More importantly, he recorded his people's and his own efforts to continue as a viable culture and people during a transitional period, 1820–90.

During this period, the Ottawa were forced to sign treaties that (1) stipulated the sale of Ottawa land, (2) advocated the removal of the Ottawas to lands west of the Mississippi River, and (3) demanded that Ottawas become "civilized." In return, rights and land were reserved for the Ottawas, they received money for education and other "civilizing" activities, and the Ottawas were guaranteed that they would be protected and treated fairly during this transitional time.

Blackbird spent a good deal of his life making sure that the state of Michigan and the federal government upheld treaty promises and guarantees. He understood that meeting the requirements of "civilization" meant getting a white man's education and becoming a citizen of the state. If Ottawas accomplished this goal, they could also remain in Michigan, near their ancestral homelands.

In 1850, Michigan granted state citizenship to "civilized" Native Americans. Blackbird was born in the early 1820s and he died in 1908, so he was not born a voting citizen but he died one. Blackbird went to Ypsilanti Normal School and held a variety of jobs from farmhand to postmaster of Harbor Springs. He demonstrated how to be a "civilized Indian" while retaining a strong sense of Ottawa identity. His history attests to his ability to adapt to changing times while remaining true to his own Ottawa family and culture.

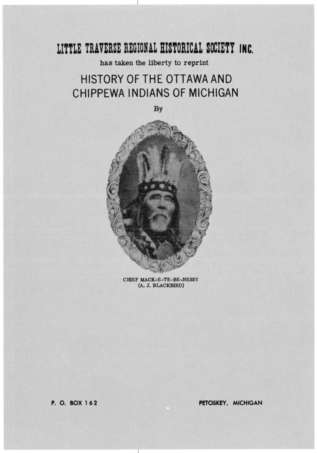

[2.9]

Source: Andrew Blackbird, *History of the Ottawa and Chippewa Indians of Michigan* (1887; reprint, Petoskey, Mich.: Little Traverse Regional Historical Society, 1967).

© PATRICK RUSSELL LEBEAU 2005 / ALL RIGHTS RESERVED

The Twenty-one Precepts or Moral Commandments of the Ottawa and Chippewa Indians, by Which They Were Governed in Their Primitive State, before They Came in Contact with White Races in Their Country

1st. Thou shalt fear the Great Creator, who is the over ruler of all things.

2nd. Thou shalt not commit any crime, either by night or by day, or in a covered place: for the Great Spirit is looking upon thee always, and thy crime shall be manifested in time, thou knowest not when, which shall be to thy disgrace and shame.

3rd. Look up to the skies often, by day and by night, and see the sun, moon and stars which shineth in the firmament, and think that the Great Spirit is looking upon thee continually.

4th. Thou shalt not mimic or mock the thunders of the cloud, for they were specially created to water the earth and to keep down all the evil monsters that are under the earth, which would eat up and devour the inhabitants of the earth if they were set at liberty.

5th. Thou shalt not mimic or mock any mountains or rivers, or any prominent formation of the earth, for it is the habitation of some deity or spirit of the earth, and thy life shall be continually in hazard if thou shouldst provoke the anger of these deities.

6th. Honor thy father and thy mother, that thy days may be long upon the land.

7th. Honor the gray-head persons, that thy head may also be like unto theirs.

8th. Thou shalt not mimic or ridicule the cripple, the lame, or deformed, for thou shall be crippled thyself like unto them if thou shouldst provoke the Great Spirit.

9th. Hold thy peace, and answer not back, when thy father or thy mother or any aged person should chastise thee for thy wrong.

10th. Thou shalt never tell a falsehood to thy parents, nor to thy neighbors, but be always upright in thy words and in thy dealings with thy neighbors.

11th. Thou shalt not steal anything from thy neighbor, nor covet anything that is his.

12th. Thou shalt always feed the hungry and the stranger.

13th. Thou shalt keep away from licentiousness and all other lascivious habits, nor utter indecent language before thy neighbor and the stranger.

© PATRICK RUSSELL LEBEAU 2005 / ALL RIGHTS RESERVED

14th.   Thou shalt not commit murder while thou art in dispute with thy neighbor, unless it be whilst on the warpath.

15th.   Thou shalt chastise thy children with the rod whilst they are in thy power.

16th.   Thou shalt disfigure thy face with charcoals, and fast at least ten days or more of each year, whilst thou are yet young, or before thou reachest twenty, that thou mayest dream of thy future destiny.

17th.   Thou shalt immerse thy body into the lake or river at least ten days in succession in the early part of the spring of the year, that thy body may be strong and swift of foot to chase the game and on the warpath.

18th.   At certain times with thy wife or thy daughters, thou shalt clean out thy fireplaces and make thyself a new fire with thy fire-sticks for the sake of thyself and for the sake of thy children's health.

19th.   Thou shalt not eat with thy wife and daughters at such time, of food cooked on a new fire, but they shall be provided with a separate kettle and cook their victuals therein with an old fire and out of their wigwam, until the time is passed, then thou shalt eat with them.

20th.   Thou shalt not be lazy, nor be a vagabond of the earth, to be hated by all men.

21st.   Thou shalt be brave, and not fear any death.

If thou shouldst observe all these commandments, when thou diest thy spirit shall go straightway to that happy land where all the good spirits are, and shall there continually dance with the beating of the drum of Tehl-baw-yaw-booz., the head spirit in the spirit land. But if thou shouldst not observe them, thy spirit shall be a vagabond of the earth always, and go hungry, and will never be able to find this road, "Tehi-bay-kon," in which all the good spirits travel.

© PATRICK RUSSELL LEBEAU 2005 / ALL RIGHTS RESERVED

[2.11] COMPANY K OF THE FIRST MICHIGAN SHARPSHOOTERS, UNION ARMY, AMERICAN CIVIL WAR, 1863–1865

Company K was composed of 150 Native Americans who served in the American Civil War between 1863 and 1865. Although the company included mostly Ottawa, Chippewa, and Ottawa-Chippewa people from the state of Michigan, other soldiers in the company were Potawatomis, Delawares, Hurons, Oneidas, and mixed-blood Native Americans. The leader of this company was Lieutenant Garret A. Gravaraet, an Ottawa schoolteacher from Little Traverse Bay, Michigan. Members of the company were recruited from Oceana and Mason Counties, Grand Traverse and Little Traverse Bays, the Saginaw Valley, and the Upper Peninsula. They came from such Michigan cities as Bay City, Grand Traverse (or Traverse City), Grand Rapids, Kalamazoo, and Northport.

Company K was designated as "sharpshooters," which means that they were considered an elite unit and had special training as skirmishers and marksmen. Company members wore the Union blue uniform of the Army of the Potomac. They fought shoulder to shoulder with white companies in the same regiment and alongside many other Union units. Company K participated in many major battles, including the Battles of Spotsylvania, the Crater, the Wilderness, and the Bloody Angle.

Even though they were living in their ancestral homeland, these Native American men were motivated to serve because their homeland had become part of the state of Michigan and the greater United States. The Native Americans had to change as a people, a community, and as a culture to accommodate this new set of circumstances. Unfortunately, many white people still coveted the Indians' lands and wanted Native Americans removed from the state because of prejudice and racism. By serving in the military, these Native American soldiers demonstrated their willingness to become a part of the greater U.S. community and showed how much they were willing to sacrifice to remain in their homeland as meaningful, loyal, and contributing members of state and Union.

Source: Charles Myers and R. D. Winthrop with Laurence M. Hauptman, *Between Two Fires: American Indians in the Civil War* (New York: Free Press, 1995), 125–44.

 © PATRICK RUSSELL LEBEAU 2005 / ALL RIGHTS RESERVED

[2.12] NARRATIVE EXPLANATION OF GLASS PLATE DAGUERREOTYPE OF PAYSON WOLFE, GRAND RIVER BAND ODAWA AND MEMBER OF COMPANY K, FIRST MICHIGAN SHARPSHOOTERS

You have been given a facsimile of a glass plate daguerreotype of Payson Wolfe, Grand River Band Odawa and member of Company K, First Michigan Sharpshooters. According to researchers, the daguerreotype was taken in Chicago in late 1863, when the First Michigan Sharpshooters were assigned to Camp Douglas as prison guards. Payson wears a greatcoat, tall dress, and Hardee hat, none of which would have lasted long after the First Michigan Sharpshooters went east to Virginia. Payson was thirty when he enlisted, older than the average recruit, and married with a family. His parents were high-status members of a Grand River band. His mother, Kinnequa, was the daughter of Waukazoo and was an herbalist of some standing. His father, Miingun (Wolf), was a warrior and *mide* (spiritual leader) who died fairly young. According to Charlie Meyers, Payson means, "I leave this thing behind." Wolfe was bilingual and literate. He graduated from Northport Mission School in Leelanau County. He was an ardent Republican and Unionist, and he almost certainly harbored deep abolitionist sentiments. He was captured by the Confederate army at Petersburg on June 17, 1864, and remained at Andersonville Prison until he was paroled in November 1864. He lived until 1900.

[2.13]

Payson Wolfe. Courtesy of the Burton Historical Collection, Detroit Public Library.

Vocabulary: A *daguerreotype* is an early photograph. The photographic process required a heavy metallic plate coated with a light-sensitive silver substance inserted into a bulky camera commonly mounted on a tripod. The subject, in this case Payson Wolfe, had to stand very still for several minutes while his impression was made on the metallic plate. The plate was then developed by mercury vapor. The "negative" could easily become scratched or broken.

Source: Charles Myers and R. D. Winthrop with Laurence M. Hauptman, *Between Two Fires: American Indians in the Civil War* (New York: Free Press, 1995), 125–44.

© PATRICK RUSSELL LEBEAU 2005 / ALL RIGHTS RESERVED

Part 1 ▸ Pontiac and Tecumseh

Activity A: Can Book Titles Influence Our Thinking?

① What is leadership? What are the characteristics of leadership?

② How do these book titles influence our thinking? What emotions, if any, do they evoke? What story do they tell in and of themselves?

③ Think of the titles as a whole. What is the major theme that connects them all? Why are there so many similarities?

④ Do you detect any definition of *leadership* in the group? If so, what words are used to indicate "leader"?

⑤ How would you define *conspiracy, massacre, rebel,* and *uprising,* and what do these words say about the authors' points of view? What do these words suggest about the character of the Indians in question?

Activity B: Images of Warriors on Book Covers

① What general theme emerges as you look at the images of Pontiac, Tecumseh, and other Indian warriors?

② Describe the demeanors, stances, and faces of Pontiac and Tecumseh. What do you imagine they are thinking?

③ What kind of clothes are they wearing? What do these clothes say about their occupation or preoccupation?

④ Can you find examples of European influences such as clothing or other material objects? What does the presence of these Western influences mean?

⑤ Did you find women or children depicted in any of the images you examined? What kind of images dominate, and how do they contribute to the books' intent and focus?

⑥ How are warriors drawn (depicted)? What similarities exist? Differences? Can you tell an Ottawa warrior from a Shawnee? How do Woodland Indian warriors differ from Sioux Indian warriors? How are they alike?

⑦ Why would an automobile manufacturer name a car division Pontiac? Are there other automobiles named after Indian warriors, Indian warrior themes, or Indian subject matter in general?

 © PATRICK RUSSELL LEBEAU 2005 / ALL RIGHTS RESERVED

Activity C: Expanding the Native American World beyond Warriors and Warfare

1. Where did Indian people live in 1763 and 1812, and where do they live today?

2. Do the Ottawas live differently than Chippewas or Potawatomis?

3. How do they differ today from 1763 and 1812? How are they alike? Can you answer these questions? Why or why not?

4. How many books did you find about the Three Fires People? How many books did you find about Indian warriors (or leaders)? What accounts for the difference (if any) in the number?

5. Look at the titles listed in the handouts "Titles of Biographies of Pontiac and Tecumseh" and "Culturally Relevant History Books." How do they differ? What does the second list convey as the focus and subjects of the books? How do the words in the titles differ?

Part 2 ▶ Pokagon and Blackbird

Activity A: Treaties and Removal

1. How did Pokagon resist removal? How were he and his people able to stay in the state of Michigan? What strategies did he develop to remain in the state? What did the Potawatomis have to do to stay?

2. Why was it so important for Pokagon and his people to remain near and around their homeland? (Think of practical and emotional reasons why you might want to stay close to your home.)

3. How can biographers counter romantic fantasies of "Great Chief" or "Great Friend of the White Man" in describing Pokagon's actions? Why? How can biographers convey to their readers the idea of ordinary Indians contributing to the welfare of their people? How can biographers create an impression of family/community? How is Pokagon less "extraordinary" than an Indian warrior such as Pontiac?

4. According to Blackbird, did U.S. government officials honor their country's treaty obligations?

5. What is the purpose of exchanging land for money, farming equipment, and an education in the "manners and customs of the white man?"

6. From the perspective of the United States, what is the definition of a "civilized" Indian?

7. Is Blackbird "civilized"? Is Pokagon "civilized"?

8. Can a Native American be "civilized" and still retain "Indian" ways?

© PATRICK RUSSELL LEBEAU 2005 / ALL RIGHTS RESERVED

Explain. What are "Indian" ways as you have encountered them in the readings? Give specific examples.

⑨ How does Blackbird show or share his Ottawa identity with his readers?

⑩ How did Michigan Native Americans avoid removal?

Activity B: The Importance of a White Man's Education to Leopold Pokagon and Andrew Blackbird

① What would motivate a Native American to get an education? (Briefly define "an education.")

② List the advantages of an education for a Native American.

③ Why would someone not want Indians to be educated?

④ Why is citizenship so important to Blackbird?

Activity C: How Do Pokagon and Blackbird Counter Stereotypical Representations of Indian People?

① Explain your understanding of Native Americans living in Michigan in the 1800s.

② After reading about Pokagon and Blackbird, do you have a different view and understanding of Indians who lived in Michigan from 1830 to 1890? Explain these differences. How do Pokagon's and Blackbird's histories change your view of Native Americans who lived in Michigan from 1830 to 1890?

③ What do the twenty-one precepts listed at the end of Blackbird's history tell you about the character of a traditional Ottawa person?

④ Write a summary of what you have learned from Pokagon and Blackbird about Indian life from 1830 to 1890.

Activity D: Leadership

① Historian James Clifton presents an alternative analysis of Michigan Indian leadership. Pokagon is not a typical "leader" as defined by most biographers and historians. What is the common definition of a leader? Why is a leader heroic? How does Pokagon differ from this ideal? Would Pokagon enjoy being singled out as special? How does he differ from your understanding of Pontiac or Tecumseh as leaders?

② Define an "Indian" leader. What is the purpose of leadership in Indian communities in the 1880s? Is being a leader for self-gratification part of the Indian definition? If so, give some examples from the readings. If not, give

 © PATRICK RUSSELL LEBEAU 2005 / ALL RIGHTS RESERVED

some examples of how, as Clifton writes, leaders, or *Wkameks*, were reminded daily that "they were no more than first among equals." Give some examples of how this statement applies to Pokagon. Think of well-known non–Native American leaders. Does "first among equals" apply to them?

③ Why does Clifton avoid the term *hero?* Why is *hero* not applicable to Pokagon or Blackbird? Does the word *hero* apply to Pontiac and Tecumseh? How can this word influence or perhaps distort our thinking?

④ Is the Western understanding of leadership (generals, kings, and statesmen) a fair way of describing Native American individuals? How? How is it not fair? Write a new definition that incorporates both Western and Native American perspectives.

Activity E: Christianity

① Does or did conversion to Christianity bestow any political or economic advantage to Native American people? If so, explain the details.

② Why did Pokagon and the Potawatomis decide not to be Baptists any longer and to convert to Catholicism?

③ Chapter 14 of Blackbird's *History of the Ottawa* has the "Twenty-one Precepts of the Ottawa and Chippewa" in English followed by the "Ten Commandments," "The Creed," and the "Lord's Prayer" in Ottawa. Are you, as a careful reader, meant to learn something from the twenty-one precepts? What kind of life (or way of life) do these precepts suggest that a person should live? Explain your answer.

④ How are the Ottawa-Chippewa precepts listed in Blackbird's history comparable to the Bible's Ten Commandments? Can a Native American be Christian and still stay true to many aspects of traditional Native American culture? Does one way of life have to exclude the other?

Part 3 ▶ Historical Juxtapositions: Three Fires People in the Civil War

Activity A: Michigan Native Americans and the American Civil War

① Is it hard to imagine Michigan Native Americans serving as soldiers in the Union army in the American Civil War? Why or why not?

② What would motivate Native Americans to serve in a military that at times during fought wars against the Three Fires people and would fight wars with Indian people west of the Mississippi between 1865 and 1900?

© PATRICK RUSSELL LEBEAU 2005 / ALL RIGHTS RESERVED

③ How does this information change your understanding of the Indian warrior depicted in many history books?

④ How does the image of Payson Wolfe influence your thinking about stereotypical images of Indian warriors?

⑤ What evidence can you draw on to demonstrate that Payson Wolfe is still an Odawa? How has he adapted to changing times? What evidence can you find in the handouts that Payson Wolfe is a loyal resident of the state of Michigan and of the Union? Explain your answer.

⑥ Are these Michigan Union soldiers not "Indian" any more because they have served? What does their service say about change and adaptation to dramatic events? Are they any less heroic or less brave for having served?

© PATRICK RUSSELL LEBEAU 2005 / ALL RIGHTS RESERVED

LESSON THE THIRD

Indian Treaties and the U.S. Constitution

MAJOR PREMISE

The U.S. Constitution guarantees and protects Michigan Indian sovereignty and treaty rights. The relationship between Indian treaties and the U.S. Constitution explicates four basic concepts about Indian treaty rights: (1) sovereignty, (2) reserved rights, (3) goods and services bought and paid for, and (4) money owed to Indian peoples for ceded lands.

OBJECTIVES

To demonstrate that:

- The Constitution recognizes sovereignty of tribal nations.
- The Constitution affirms that treaties are the supreme law of the land; therefore, treaties (which establish tribal governments and reserved lands and rights within states) and tribes (whose people live within the states) are not directly under the states' jurisdiction or laws.
- Indian people are owed a great deal of money as compensation for land.
- Indians have bought and paid for many goods and services, such as the education of future generations of Indian people.
- Indians have reserved land and rights for their exclusive use. What was not sold is retained as rights and privileges.
- Indians have sovereignty and the right to be self-governing on their reserved lands. No other people within the boundaries of the United States have signed treaties with the federal government, and no other people have their own governments and recognized land base.

Lesson the Third details the relationship between Indian treaties and the U.S. Constitution. Article 1, section 8, of the U.S. Constitution forms the basis for tribal sovereignty, and Article 6, paragraph 2 establishes that "all treaties made . . . shall be the Supreme law of the land" (3.1). Therefore, the U.S. Constitution recognizes tribal governments and land held in common. Furthermore, the rights, money, and privileges guaranteed and promised in treaties for the exchange of Indian land are protected and honored by the U.S. Constitution. Constitutional principles, such as the rule of law and checks and balances, are explored by looking at select federal court cases regarding the validity and legality of Indian treaties. State governments and the legislative and the executive branches of the U.S. government have, over the years, challenged Indian treaties and have passed laws limiting or extinguishing rights written in the treaties as promises and payments for land. Indians have often had to sue these governments in federal court to get these rights back. The articles of the U.S. Constitution mentioned earlier provide ample reason for judicial reversal of laws deemed to violate Indian treaties.

Therefore, this lesson answers a few basic questions: Why can Indians build gambling casinos? Why do select members of federally recognized Indian tribes have the right to fish without state or federal licenses or to attend state-funded institutions of higher education free of tuition?

A treaty is a formal agreement and legal contract between two or more sovereign states. A treaty is also the official document in which such an agreement is set down. Most Indian treaties, as legal contracts, outline the terms for the exchange of money, services, reserved rights, peace, and other promises for Indian land. In *Pathfinding: An Introduction to Indian Treaty Law*, an out-of-print booklet, Michigan Native American attorney, Michael Petoskey, writes, "A treaty is a legal agreement between two or more sovereign nations. . . . The U.S. made treaties with Indians to end wars and to get more lands for settlement. At the same time, Indians used treaties to keep their rights, [such as] the right of self government" (13). Bill Church, a former Michigan Native American educator, explains in his introduction to the same text, "Treaties are a roadmap [that allows] for the exploration of both [Michigan's] beginning history and the history of its First People." Dr. George Cornell, Native American and director of Michigan State University's Native American Institute, writes in that treaties are "legal agreements [that] gave Indian lands to the federal government. Other purposes . . . included making tribal boundaries, setting up Indian reservations, and reserving Indian fishing and hunting rights" (9). More importantly, by the act of creating treaties with Indians, the federal government recognized, in an official and legal way, the sovereign and separate governments of the Indian tribes.

Native American leaders signed treaties to protect their descendants' rights and livelihoods. By 1835, Native Americans understood the power of the U.S. government and its military: but more preferred British contacts, especially since many Michigan Indians received annual presents from the British until 1848. Indians understood that they no longer had the military or economic power to challenge the United States. Signing treaties was a way of at least retaining rights, privileges, land, and homes within the state. Native American leaders also negotiated for payment for lands. Native American treaty signers also negotiated the important issue of education for their people, showing that these leaders understood that the world was changing and would be different for future generations. These Native Americans knew that their people needed skills and training to adapt to this new world. The continuing presence of strong, viable, and growing Native American communities within the state proves nineteenth-century Native Americans' wisdom in negotiating and signing treaties.

Looking at Indian treaties in a very simple way, most students can identify four basic principles. (1) Treaties recognize the sovereignty and governments of Indian tribes. (2) Treaties allow Native Americans to keep rights and privileges such as reserved land and hunting and fishing rights. (3) Because the United States was technically buying Indian land, payment, in the form of money and promises, was given at the time of the "contract" signing and for many years thereafter. (4) The U.S. government promised to protect the welfare and rights of Native American people.

In 1787, the U.S. Constitution was adopted. Article 1, Section 8, grants Congress the power "to regulate commerce with foreign nations, and among the several states, and with Indian tribes." This statement means that Indian nations have the same status and sovereignty as states and foreign nations (Michigan or France, for example) except that the U.S. government had and has plenary power over Indian affairs but not necessarily over Indian treaty rights.

VOCABULARY

- *Plenary* means complete in all respects, unlimited, or full (American Heritage Dictionary).
- *Sovereignty* is supremacy of authority or rule as exercised by a sovereign or sovereign state, royal rank, authority, or power as well as complete independence and self-government. In addition, *sovereignty* is defined as a territory existing as an independent state (American Heritage Dictionary).

Despite their sovereign status, Indian nations within the borders of the United States are not "foreign states" because their lands "compose a part of the

United States." Chief Justice John Marshall, in his 1831 Supreme Court decision in *Cherokee Nation v. Georgia*, wrote that an Indian nation is a "domestic, dependent nation" with "a distinct political society . . . capable of managing its own affairs and governing itself." Because of the Indian treaties with the United States, foreign nations and the U.S. government consider Indian nations within U.S. borders "completely under the sovereignty and domination of the United States." This means that tribal governments are like state governments and cannot make agreements or treaties with foreign nations. Tribes have sovereignty, but that sovereignty is limited by the boundaries of the United States, the U.S. Constitution, and the federal government.

IMPORTANT CONCEPTS I

In *Worcester v. Georgia* (1831), Chief Justice John Marshall defined the relationship between Indian nations and the U.S. and state governments. This relationship is explained by the following terms:

- *Plenary power* means that only the federal government can negotiate with Indian nations. Individuals and state (or other local) governments cannot directly negotiate with Indians. The federal government is responsible for creating legislation affecting Indian affairs. However, these negotiations and laws must not violate the U.S. Constitution.
- *Trust relationship* means that the federal government must protect Indian tribes in the same manner that parents protect and look out for the welfare and safety of their children.
- *Reserved rights* means that Indians have the full right and power to self-govern, to hold land in common on "reserved lands," and to hunt, gather, and fish on ceded lands.

Exclusion of state law from Indian-held lands means that an Indian tribe "is a distinct community, occupying its own territory, with boundaries accurately described, in which the laws of [Michigan] can have no force" (Chief Justice John Marshall, *Worcester v. Georgia* [1831]).

Furthermore, states, including Michigan, cannot pass laws that violate, amend, or abrogate Indian treaties because they are the "supreme law of the land." Treaties are, in this sense, sanctioned and protected by the U.S. Constitution. States can pass laws as long as they do not violate the U.S. Constitution. Article 6, paragraph 2, of the U.S. Constitution, states,

This constitution, and the laws of the United States which shall be made in pursuance thereof; and all treaties made, or which shall be made, under authority of the United States shall be the Supreme law of the land; and the judges in every state shall be bound thereby, anything in the constitution or laws of any state to the contrary notwithstanding.

This article reserved for the United States the power to make treaties with Indian nations and prevented states from interfering with this process. The purpose of treaties with Indian nations was to acquire land in a legal and proper manner while protecting the rights of Indian people.

Most treaties were negotiated after many years of warfare, disease, and other economic and social pressures had weakened and in some cases virtually destroyed Indian nations' cultural, social, and familial structures. In this way, Indian nations were forced to negotiate and sign treaties. This does not mean, however, that Indian nations lost everything. Treaties protected Native Americans from total annihilation. In many cases, treaties reserved ancestral lands for Indians' exclusive use or provided funds to purchase nearby lands for the Indians' exclusive use. Other rights—fishing and hunting, for example— were also reserved. Money, food, agricultural equipment, and other services were exchanged for the valuable land Indians were forced to cede to the United States. Therefore, Indians *retain* these rights, privileges, services, and land: nothing is *given* to them. After all, to acquire Indian land in an ethical and legal way, the United States had to pay some modicum of valuation so that the federal government, the state governments, and private citizens could enjoy the economic benefits of Indian land.

To get legal title to land in a systematic and controlled manner, treaties were necessary. Treaty documents enabled the federal government to act as the central clearinghouse for the acquisition and then redistribution of Indian land to citizens and immigrants. Therefore, treaties are state-building instruments. The maps of treaty boundaries (found in the appended resources for Lesson the Fourth) show the systematic acquisition of the lands used to create the state of Michigan and thereby illustrate this point. Each portion of land was acquired through "purchase." What was paid—some money, promises of education, reserved lands, and reserved rights—seemed very cheap from the perspective of federal treaty negotiators. Land was usually purchased for 2 to 5 cents an acre from Indians and sold for $1.25 to $2.50 per acre. The U.S paid the Revolutionary War debt by acquiring and selling Indian land.

Despite the low cost of Indian lands revealed in treaty documents, state governments and the congressional and executive branches of the U.S. government have challenged treaties and treaty rights. States, including Michigan, have tried to limit or abolish Indian rights within their boundaries. For example, Michigan challenged the right of Indians to fish in ancestral waters. In addition, Congress has enacted laws to terminate Indian nations or to limit Indian nations' ability to govern themselves. The executive and judicial branches of the U.S. government have often had to intervene to protect and uphold Indian people's rights. Without written treaties to protect them, Indians might very well have lost everything.

Major Supreme Court decisions, like Chief Justice John Marshall's decisions mentioned earlier, have upheld treaties as the "supreme law of the land." These decisions have also established what historians have called the canons of construction, which establish two important rules of interpretation:

1. If any confusion in interpretation of articles or intent of articles in treaties arises, they must be interpreted to favor Indians.
2. Because treaties were negotiated and written in English, a language Indians did not understand, treaties must be interpreted as the Indians would have understood them.

IMPORTANT CONCEPTS 2

- *Canon* is an established principle, a basis for judgment, and a standard or criterion.
- *Ceded territory* refers to specific lands or territories sold in treaties. Treaty rights to hunt, fish, and gather can be exercised in the ceded territory under tribal regulation.
- *Reservation* is the land owned by an Indian tribe and is now considered the tribe's homeland. This land is often described and reserved in treaties.
- *Treaty* is a formal agreement between two or more countries or sovereign governments.

TREATY RIGHTS AND THE U.S. CONSTITUTION TIMELINE (3.1)

This timeline shows most of the congressional acts and laws, Supreme Court decisions, treaties relevant to Michigan's Indians, and other cases, decisions, and legal interpretations regarding Indian treaty law. Article 6, paragraph 2, of the U.S. Constitution receives significant placement to show why Indians of the state of Michigan have retained and reserved rights and privileges not necessarily enjoyed by the average U.S. citizen. This chart also seeks to remind students that most Indians possess dual citizenship—they are U.S. citizens as well as citizens of a particular tribe.

Indian Treaties: Relevant Information (3.4) and Indian Treaties and Michigan Indian Education (3.13)

Students will use this information to determine and evaluate Indian treaties and Indian treaty law. Each lesson plan relies on this fund of knowledge to help clarify the complexities inherent in the interpretation of Indian treaties. Students cannot thoroughly analyze Indian treaties without this information. This information also encourages students to view all the lesson plans as a whole and as related (and relevant) to one another. Therefore, students can draw from a body of relevant material to provide perspectives on many similar issues that on the surface may not appear to be at all related to Indian treaties.

The handouts provide information relevant to the general topic of Indian treaty making and law. Students should be encouraged to independently research Indian legal and treaty issues and bring the material to class for discussion. An example would be to have students look into any current local issues such as the establishment of a casino or a fishing rights dispute. The relevant information handout enables students to do as complete an analysis of Indian law as the short time set aside for each lesson plan allows.

Treaty with the Indian People of _____ Class (3.13)

This is a simplified version of an Indian treaty. The purpose is to explore the basic tenets of most treaties during the land cession period of treaty making.

The maps found in Lesson the Fourth are very useful for the activities in this lesson. Graphically, the maps from Lesson the Fourth show treaty boundaries, the locations of reserved lands, the locations of tribal governments, and other useful information. Use them in conjunction with the activities that follow.

PART 1 ▶ SOVEREIGNTY OF TRIBAL GOVERNMENTS

Introduction

The ability of Michigan's Indians to self-govern, set up gambling casinos, and have their own common land base has confused many people. Why do Indians have these rights when no one else does? The answer is that Indians are not the only people with these powers. We all have them in the form of our U.S. and state governments. For example, Congress could pass a law legalizing casino gambling, and the state of Michigan has a limited legalized gambling system in the form of the lottery. The federal government owns "public land" in every state in the Union, and the state of Michigan owns land as well. Public lands belong to every U.S. citizen; state-held lands can be said to belong to the citizens of that state.

Confusion arises when we mistake the rights of individual people with the rights of governments. The U.S. government, state governments, and tribal governments are separate entities within the overall makeup of the United States of America. Each government can create laws and regulate activities within its jurisdiction. The U.S. government is supreme and makes laws and regulations by which states and tribes must abide, but the U.S. government allows states and tribes a great deal of autonomy. States and tribes, however, cannot separate themselves from the U.S. government to negotiate with foreign nations, for example. Our central federal government has the exclusive right to act on behalf of the nation as whole. State governments act on behalf of their citizens. Therefore, if one state wants casino gambling, the choice is up to the voters of that state. Tribal governments have similar rights, privileges, and responsibilities. Tribal governments act on behalf and with the consent of tribal members. This ability and right to establish a government are key to understanding the concept of sovereignty.

So, when you think of why Indians have rights and privileges, think of governments. You have rights and privileges as both a citizen of the United States and a citizen of your state. Some of Michigan's Indian people are citizens of the United States, the state of Michigan, and their tribes. The sovereignty of Michigan's Indian tribes is recognized and validated by Michigan's Indian treaties.

Objectives

- To understand the importance of Michigan's Indian treaties as binding promises; as validating documentation for reserved rights, special privileges, and self-government; and as contracting agreements for the exchange of land for specified compensation.
- To explore the meaning of *sovereignty* as it applies to Michigan's Indian governments.
- To demonstrate how Indian treaties have the backing of the U.S. Constitution and are the supreme law of the land.
- To show how treaties, like the Constitution, are enduring and living documents that protect the rights of Indian people.

① Prepare "Treaty Rights and the U.S. Constitution" (3.1) and "Timeline" (3.2) handouts for each student or student group or display the chart itself so that students have easy access. Read the timeline or have students read the timeline at least once: have students study closely the highlighted words.

② Prepare "Sovereignty of Tribal Governments: Basic Vocabulary and Introduction" handouts (3.3) and have students read the introduction, or read it to the class as a whole.

③ Prepare and have students read "Relevant Information: Indian Treaties" handout (3.4). Instruct students to refer to this handout when answering questions on Indian tribal sovereignty.

④ Photocopy the definitions of *sovereignty, exclusion, treaty, cede,* and *jurisdiction* (3.3 and 3.5) and distribute to students or student groups.

⑤ Have students search for major issues (for example constitutional principles, definitions of important terms) in handouts 3.1 through 3.6 to familiarize themselves with the context. Search and find the following: Article 1, section 8, and Article 6, paragraph 2, of the U.S. Constitution; Northwest Ordinance; 1836 Treaty of Washington; Boldt decision; *California et al. v. Cabazon Band;* sovereignty; treaty; and jurisdiction.

Activity A ▶ The Meaning of Sovereignty: Article 1, Section 8, U.S. Constitution

Questions for Thought and Discussion

① What are treaties? How can a treaty be proof that Indian tribes have (or possess) sovereignty?

② Read Article 1, section 8, of the U.S. Constitution (3.1). This is the accepted source establishing the sovereignty of Indian tribes. Write a paragraph explaining the context into which Indian tribes are put. Is the conjunction *and* important?

Activity B ▶ Sovereignty, Government, and Jurisdiction

Questions for Thought and Discussion

① A government of a nation or state is necessary for a sovereignty to exist. Why?

② For the most part, a land base, with borders, is necessary to exercise jurisdiction. Why?

③ The U.S. government has jurisdiction over every person and government within the borders of the United States but not, for the most part, over any person or government outside its borders. The same can be said for each state. Explain why this is also true for Indian tribes.

④ If Indian tribes have land bases and governments within the boundaries of a state, why cannot a state exercise state jurisdiction over Indian tribes?

Activity C ▶ Exploring the Treaty Rights and the U.S. Constitution Timeline

Preparation

① Explore the timeline, especially the highlighted areas. Review "Relevant Information: Indian Treaties" and "Major Michigan Indian Treaties."

Questions for Thought and Discussion

① Identify acts, cases, bills, and other declarations that demonstrate, affirm, or provide examples of Indian sovereignty. How do Indian tribes exercise the power of self-government?

② Also, in addition or separately, find those incidents where Indian sovereignty is challenged.

③ Summarize what has been learned.

PART 2 ▶ INDIAN TREATIES AS SUPREME LAW OF THE LAND: ARTICLE 6, PARAGRAPH 2, U.S. CONSTITUTION

Introduction

Treaties are artifacts from the past, primary sources for the historical exploration of Indian history. However, treaties are also living documents. Treaties are as valid today as the day the signatures at the bottom of each treaty first dried. You can compare this to how the U.S. Constitution is just as valid and relevant to Americans living today as it was to those Americans living in 1789. The Constitution defines our way of life, establishes our governmental system, and grants and protects our rights and privileges as U.S. citizens. Likewise, Indian treaties define Indians as a self-governing, land-based people with special rights and privileges. Treaties are also protected and enforced by our Constitution under Article 6, paragraph 2, which states that treaties are the "Supreme law of the land."

- To understand the importance of Michigan's Indian treaties as binding promises; as validating documentation for reserved rights, special privileges, and self-government; and as contracting agreements for the exchange of land for specified compensation.
- To explore the meaning of *sovereignty* as it applies to Michigan's Indian governments.
- To demonstrate how Indian treaties have the backing of the Constitution of the United States of America and are the Supreme Law of the Land.
- To show how treaties are like the Constitution. They are enduring and living documents that protect the rights of Native American people.

Preparation

1. Read the introduction to "Indian Treaties as Supreme Law of the Land: Basic Vocabulary, Introduction and Major Court Cases and Decisions" (3.4). Then provide the class with copies of the introduction or read it to the class as a whole.
2. Provide copies and have students read the "Relevant Information: Indian Treaties" (3.3) and "Indians Treaties as Supreme Law of the Land: Basic Vocabulary, Introduction and Major Court Cases and Decisions" (3.4). Instruct students to refer to these handouts when answering questions on Indian tribal sovereignty.
3. Be sure students have studied the dictionary definitions of *government, sovereignty, treaty, cede,* and *jurisdiction.*
4. Have handouts of "Treaty Rights and the U.S. Constitution Timeline" (3.1) or use the chart itself positioned so that students can read the information at a glance or without too much trouble. Read the timeline at least once, and have students study closely the highlighted words.

Activity A ▶ The Supreme Law of the Land

Questions for Thought and Discussion

1. What does the "supreme law of the land" mean?
2. Can anyone break this law? Amend this law?
3. How does "supreme law of the land" validate the special rights and privileges of Indian tribes and people?

Preparation

① Explore the timeline, especially the highlighted areas. Review "Relevant Information: Indian Treaties" (3.4).

Questions for Thought and Discussion

① Identify acts, cases, bills, or other declarations that demonstrate, affirm, or provide examples of how treaties are the "supreme law of the land."

② The state of Michigan and some individuals have challenged the legal force of Indian treaties. Find those cases on the timeline (or on the Internet or in newspaper articles) and write a short paragraph explaining why the Supreme Court was compelled to uphold the rights of Indian tribes.

PART 3 ▶ NEGOTIATING AN INDIAN TREATY

Introduction

An Indian treaty is a written contract between the U.S. government and a specific Indian nation. After negotiations are concluded, representatives of each party sign the document. This makes this contract legal and binding.

Objectives

- To understand the importance of Michigan's Indian treaties as binding promises; as validating documentation for reserved rights, special privileges, and self-government; and as contracting agreements for the exchange of land for specified compensation.
- To show how treaties, like the U.S. Constitution, are enduring and living documents that protect the rights of Indian people.

Preparation

① Divide the class as follows:
  - 75 percent (or most) of the class will be challengers (people who do not agree with one or more treaty articles);
  - 10 percent of the class (or at least 3 students) represent the Indian tribe;

- 5 percent of the class (or at least 1 or 2 students) are the U.S. government's treaty-making officials;
- 5 percent of the class (or at least 1 or 2 students) are interpreters (people who can speak English as well as "Indian");
- 5 percent of the class (or at least 1 or 2 students) are Supreme Court justices (to settle any disputes).

❷ Have students (except for challengers and Indians) study Article 1, section 8, and Article 6, paragraph 2, of the U.S. Constitution (3.1). Supreme Court justices should know these articles well and have a clear understanding of the canons of construction (3.4).

❸ Distribute copies of the student handouts, "Negotiating an Indian Treaty" (3.8 through 3.12) and "Treaty with the Indian People of _____ Class" (3.13).

❹ Assume that the class as a whole is Indian land for the moment, except for the teacher's desk and enough space close to the teacher's desk for Supreme Court justices (and their desks).

Activity A ▶ Role-Playing Treaty Negotiations

The activity starts with the treaty negotiations between the Indian tribe and government officials, with the interpreters facilitating communication between the two groups. The rest of the class watches. (Use the "Treaty with the Indian People of _____ Class" [3.13] or create your own.) Once each group's objectives are met, the challengers move into "Indian Land" and prepare their document. From there, the Supreme Court is petitioned to hear the case of challengers versus Indians. The justices then make a decision based on the documents submitted and on their understanding of the U.S. Constitution and other rulings made by historical Supreme Court justices on similar cases.

❶ General Instructions for Indian Tribe: Most of the Indian land base will be taken away from you whether you like it or not. Your goal is to get something in exchange for that land without a heated confrontation. You want: (1) some land set aside for your permanent use and guaranteed to be yours forever; (2) hunting, fishing, and gathering rights so that your people will have food; and (3) guarantees that the government will provide for the education of your children and their descendants. You should also create pictographs (small drawings of animals, objects found in nature, or anything else you can imagine); these will be your signatures. You must also draft a response to the challengers and submit it to the Supreme Court. Your response must include the reasons you think they are wrong.

② General Instructions for U.S. Government Officials: Your goal is to get the Indians to sign the treaty. You are open to most proposals that do not cost a lot of money. You also realize that these Indian people need at least some land. You can negotiate how much, although your goal is to get as much of the land as possible. Confine the Indians to the space (the part of the classroom) you have set aside for them. You should agree to anything that does not cost money. You want to pay some money for the land you are getting. You have a budget of $1 million. However, you want to spend this money on items and services that will "civilize" the Indian people rather than giving out cash. You also help the interpreters draft the treaty and make sure everyone signs.

③ General Instructions for Interpreters: You are to convey each party's desires and proposals to the other party. They are not allowed to speak directly to one another. Try your best to be accurate. You also determine when the negotiations are over. You help write out the treaty. You can either use the mock treaty provided or use the mock treaty as a pattern for writing your own.

④ General Instructions for Challengers: You move into the areas of the classroom not occupied by Indians. After the treaty is signed, you decide on one article (or part of the treaty) that you will dispute. You must compose a short paper identifying the article and explaining why you do not like it. Submit your paper to the Supreme Court.

⑤ General Instructions for Supreme Court Justices: Review the challengers' paper and the Indians' response. Based on your understanding of treaties, the articles relevant to treaties in the Constitution, and the canons of construction, decide who you think is right and write out an explanation of why you reached that decision.

Questions for Thought and Discussion

① What problems did you encounter or witness as the two parties tried to negotiate and sign a treaty?

② Do the interpreters get in the way? Could you have accomplished your task more easily without them?

③ No matter what the Indians negotiate for, why do they still lose out?

④ Who do the challengers represent in real life? Why might they have some grievance or dispute with the Indian treaty?

⑤ Do the Supreme Court justices have to decide in favor of the Indians? Why or why not?

⑥ How do you make promises? Do you keep them? Are you obligated to honor them? Is a moral code part of the idea behind making promises?

⓻ If you make a promise in writing and sign your name to that written promise, is the promise more important? Does your signature add validity to your promise?

Activity B ▶ Exploring "Treaty with the Indian People of _____ Class"

Questions for Thought and Discussion

① Article the First: What does this article mean? How do you define the words *peace, friendship,* and *perpetual?*

② Article the Second: What do Indians get in return for "ceding and relinquishing" all their land? Do they in fact "give" away "all" of their land?

③ Article the Third: This is the payment clause. Is money the only currency of exchange? Money is stipulated to buy goods and services. What is the nature of these goods and services? How do they help Indian people? What are they designed to accomplish?

④ Article the Fourth: Why does the U.S. government want to "protect the rights" of Indian people? What does *protect* mean? Why is it important? Does this mean that the U.S. government can harm or fully control the rights of Indian people?

Activity C ▶ Four Concepts Inherent in Indian Treaties

① The act of negotiating and signing a treaty recognizes tribal sovereignty and government. Native American tribal governments, like state governments, can govern themselves and pass laws as long as they do not violate the U.S. Constitution.

② Native Americans reserved land as well as hunting and fishing rights. This is where the term *reservation* originates.

③ The U.S. government paid money and promised to provide numerous goods and services in exchange for Indian land. In this sense, Indian education and health care are "goods and services" bought and paid for in advance by the sale of Indian land.

④ The U.S. government promised to "protect the rights" of Native American people and governments.

Questions for Thought and Discussion

① Which concept makes casino gambling possible?

② The Michigan Indian Tuition Waiver falls under which category?

③ Which category allows for commercial fishing by recognized tribal members?

④ Why did federal courts reverse restrictions and prohibitions against Indian fishing and gambling operations?

PART 4 ▶ TRIBES, STATES, AND THE U.S. GOVERNMENT: TREATY RIGHTS LOST AND WON BACK

Introduction

Despite sovereignty and the protection of the U.S. Constitution, treaties have not always been honored or interpreted to the advantage of Native American people. States and individuals have tried to interfere, ignore, and challenge the rights of Indian tribes. Even Congress has enacted legislation to limit Indian treaty rights. Courts at every level have heard many cases involving Indian treaty rights, for the most part ruling in favor of Indian tribes. Using the concepts of Indian tribal sovereignty, treaties as the supreme law of the land, and the canons of construction (concepts explored in the lesson plans preceding this one), courts make decisions favoring Indian treaty rights. Education, fishing, and casino gambling are rights for which Michigan's Indians have had to fight in the courts. The Indian tribes used Michigan's Indian treaties to prove their cases and regain rights that many other people sought to deny to the Native Americans.

Objectives

- To understand the importance of Michigan's Indian treaties as binding promises; as validating documentation for reserved rights, special privileges, and self-government; and as contracting agreements for the exchange of land for specified compensation.
- To explore the meaning of *sovereignty* as it applies to Michigan's Indian governments.
- To demonstrate how Indian treaties have the backing of the U.S. Constitution and are the supreme law of the land.
- To show how treaties, like the U.S. Constitution, are enduring and living documents that protect the rights of Indian people.

1. Prepare copies of "Relevant Information: Indian Treaties" (3.4), "Michigan Indian Education" (3.14), and "Major Michigan Indian Treaties" (3.6) to students.

2. Be sure that students have studied the dictionary definitions of *government*, *sovereign*, *treaty*, *cede*, and *jurisdiction*.

3. Prepare copies of the "Treaty Rights and the U.S. Constitution Timeline." Have students read the timeline at least once and have them study closely the highlighted words.

4. Review the canons of construction.

Activity A ▶ Indian Education as a Specific Compensation for Ceded Land: The Michigan Indian Tuition Waiver Act ("Michigan Indian Education" [3.14])

1. The 1836 Treaty of Washington between the United States and the Ottawas and Chippewas and the 1855 Treaty of Detroit between U.S. government and the Ottawas and Chippewas included provisions for Indian education in what would later become the state of Michigan. However, many Michigan Native Americans initially resisted government-imposed education as a form of pressure to abandon tribal customs.

2. Indian education was the responsibility of the federal government's Bureau of Indian Affairs (BIA).

3. Mission boarding schools, day schools, and public schools (before 1888) failed as methods of educating Native American children.

4. Manual labor training (MLT) schools were established in the state of Michigan between 1888 and 1893. These schools provided technical training for Native American youths throughout the state.

5. These MLT schools were closed in the 1930s. The land and buildings were given to the state of Michigan in exchange for educating Michigan's Indians as promised and stipulated in U.S. treaties with the same Indians.

6. The state of Michigan did not honor this promise until 1976, when Native Americans fought for and won the right to free public education, including college tuition at state-supported institutions. As of this writing, Native American people who can prove Indian blood quantum, according to federal guidelines, can attend Michigan's public institutions of higher learning tuition-free. Some of the institutions, like the University of Michigan, do not admit the validity of this principle, and choose to grant a scholarship equal to the tuition fee. While earning his Ph.D. degree at the University of

Michigan, the author's tuition was paid by such an arrangement. He did not receive the tuition waiver guaranteed by the state.

Questions for Thought and Discussion

1. Explain in your own words why Native Americans get "free" tuition. Is the tuition really "free"? Is this fair? Explain why or why not.
2. Should this promise to provide for the education of Michigan's Indians have been honored before 1976? Why or why not?
3. Why would education be important to Native American people?

Activity B ▶ Fishing: A Reserved Right

Questions for Thought and Discussion

1. Based on the information provided to you and on the "Treaty Rights and the U.S. Constitution Timeline," why do Michigan's Indians to this day have a right to fish on ceded lands?
2. Why would the Indian signers of the treaties want to keep fishing and hunting and gathering (of wild rice, berries, or maple syrup, for example) as a reserved right? What purpose would it serve?
3. Studying your answer to question 2, you have probably come up with several practical reasons why Indian people would want to fish, hunt, and gather. But that was in the past. Can you come up with practical reasons for hunting and fishing and gathering in Michigan today? Are they the same as or different from your answers to question 2? Explain. Can you contemplate any modern reasons to fish? If so, explain.

Activity C ▶ Casino Gambling: An Act of Self-Government Derived from Tribal Sovereignty, Self-Determination, and Jurisdiction

Questions for Thought and Discussion

1. Study the "Treaty Rights and the U.S. Constitution Timeline" (3.1). What legislation supports the concept of self-determination and self-government as applied to the Indian tribes of Michigan?
2. Why do or why can Indian tribes have governments? Is a land base important for this ability to self-govern? Explain.
3. Casino gambling is arguably not a traditional activity of Indian tribes. Why is this an invalid argument for restricting Indian tribes' ability to operate casinos?

④ How are treaties involved in establishing the right of Indian tribes to set up casino gambling on their tribal lands?

PART 5 ▶ INDIAN TREATIES: EXPLORING A REAL TREATY

Introduction

The 1836 Treaty of Washington between the U.S. government and some of Michigan's Indians is a very important document. In this lesson, students will read a portion of this treaty to search for articles and passages that support the themes and issues explored in the previous four sections.

Objectives

- To understand the importance of Michigan's Indian treaties as binding promises; as validating documentation for reserved rights, special privileges, and self-government; and as contracting agreements for the exchange of land for specified compensation.
- To explore the meaning of *sovereignty* as it applies to Michigan's Indian governments.
- To demonstrate how Indian treaties have the backing of the U.S. Constitution and are the supreme law of the land.
- To show how treaties, like the Constitution, are enduring and living documents that protect the rights of Indian people.

Preparation

① Read the "Facsimile of Treaty with the Ottawa and Chippewa, March 28, 1836" (3.15).
② Review all appended resources.

Questions for Thought and Discussion

① Where does the treaty set aside land for Ottawas and Chippewas? Can you figure out where in the state of Michigan these lands are located? Is this land held in common?

② Where does the treaty discuss hunting and fishing rights? What does the phrase "until the land is required for settlement" mean to you? What if the land is never required for settlement?

③ Is any money given out? If so, to whom? Why?

④ Explain in your own words what other provisions this treaty includes. Explain the meaning of *improvements*. Why do the Indians need blacksmiths or gunsmiths?

APPENDED RESOURCES

(3.1) Treaty Rights and the U.S. Constitution 98
(3.2) Timeline 99

Part 1: Sovereignty
(3.3) Sovereignty of Tribal Governments: Basic Vocabulary
and Introduction 104
(3.4) Relevant Information: Indian Treaties 106

Part 2: Supreme Law of the Land
(3.5) Indian Treaties as Supreme Law of the Land: Basic Vocabulary,
Introduction, and Major Court Cases and Decisions (3.4) 107
(3.6) Major Michigan Indian Treaties 109

Part 3: Negotiating a Real Treaty
(3.7) Negotiating an Indian Treaty: Teacher Master 111
(3.8) Negotiating an Indian Treaty: Interpreters 113
(3.9) Negotiating an Indian Treaty: U.S. Government Officials 114
(3.10) Negotiating an Indian Treaty: Supreme Court Justices 115
(3.11) Negotiating an Indian Treaty: Indian Tribe 117
(3.12) Negotiating an Indian Treaty: Challengers 118
(3.13) Treaty with the Indian People of _____ Class 119

Part 4: Indian Treaties

(3.14) Michigan Indian Education 120

Part 5: Portion of a Real Treaty

(3.15) Treaty with the Ottawa and Chippewa, March 28, 1836 121

(3.16) Questions for Thought and Discussion 123

[3.1]   TREATY RIGHTS AND THE U.S. CONSTITUTION

Constitution of the United States of America, Article 1, Section 8

Grants Congress the power "to regulate commerce with foreign nations, and among the several States, and with the Indian tribes."

Constitution of the United States of America, Article 6, Paragraph 2

This constitution, and the laws of the United States which shall be made in pursuance thereof; and all treaties made, or which shall be made, under authority of the United States shall be the Supreme law of the land; and the judges in every state shall be bound thereby, anything in the constitution or laws of any state to the contrary notwithstanding.

© PATRICK RUSSELL LEBEAU 2005 / ALL RIGHTS RESERVED

1620   *December 21.* The Mayflower lands at Plymouth Rock.

1754   At the Albany Congress, English colonists discuss a unified colonial
        Indian policy and draft the Albany Plan of Union. The social-
        political organization of the Iroquois Six-Nation Confederacy
        provides the model for this, the American colonists' first attempt
        to form a democratic government.

1763   *May 7.* Pontiac (an Ottawa) and many other outraged Indian peo-
        ple, including Ottawas, Chippewas, and Potawatomis of Michigan,
        form an alliance to attack English forts on the Old Northwest fron-
        tier. Their outrage stems from American colonists' settlement on
        Indian land and unfair trade practices.

1764   *October 7.* Royal proclamation reserves for Indians the territory
        between Appalachian Mountains and the Mississippi River. The
        proclamation also forbids American colonists to enter into or settle
        on Indian lands west of the Appalachians.

1768   Treaty of Fort Stanwix declares the Ohio River is boundary for
        white settlement. Land Northwest of the Ohio River remains Indian
        country.

1775   Continental Congress names Indian commissioners for the northern,
        middle, and southern Indian departments. Commissioners are
        authorized to make treaties with Indian tribes and to arrest British
        agents.

1775–83 Revolutionary War. Indians fought mainly on the British side to pre-
        vent American settlement on Indian lands.

1777   Articles of Confederation adopted.

1778   Delaware nation signs the first Indian treaty with the United States
        at Fort Pitt. The treaty guarantees Delaware land rights: the Ohio
        River boundary establishes peace and friendship between the
        Delaware and the newly formed U.S. government, and promised the
        Delaware a separate state in the Union.

1787   Northwest Ordinance is enacted: "The utmost good faith shall
        always be reserved for the Indians; their lands and properties shall
        never be taken from them without their consent and in their prop-
        erty rights and liberty, they shall never be invaded or disturbed."

1787   *September 17.* U.S. Constitution is adopted.

1790   Trade and Intercourse Acts regulate trade between federal govern-
        ment and Indians.

1794   First Indian Treaty signed that includes provisions for the education of
        Indians, though education was imposed as a form of indoctrination.

© PATRICK RUSSELL LEBEAU 2005 / ALL RIGHTS RESERVED

1794	Great Britain and United States sign the Jay Treaty, which recognizes sovereignty of Indian tribes, and provided for withdrawal of British troops from Mackinac Island, Detroit, and Maumee River in 1796.
1802	U.S. Congress appropriates $10,000–$15,000 annually to promote "civilization" among the Indians.
1807	*November 17.* U.S. government signs Treaty of Detroit with the Ottawas, Chippewas, Wyandots, and Potawatomis. This treaty sells (cedes) large portions of what is now southeastern Michigan. Although the land is sold, tribes keep the right to hunt, fish, and gather on ceded lands "until the land is required for settlement."
1819	*September 24.* U.S. government signs Treaty of Saginaw with the Chippewas. This treaty sells large portions of what is now the middle part of Michigan's Lower Peninsula. Although the land is sold, tribes keep the right to hunt, fish, and gather on ceded lands "until the land is required for settlement."
1821	*August 29.* U.S. government signs Treaty of Chicago with the Chippewas, Ottawas, and Potawatomis. This treaty sells large portions of what is now the southwestern Lower Peninsula. Although the land is sold, tribes keep the right to hunt, fish, and gather on ceded lands until sold to U.S. citizens.
1828	*September 20.* U.S. government signs treaty with the Potawatomis that sells land in extreme southwestern Michigan. Although the land is sold, tribes keep the right to hunt, fish, and gather on ceded lands until sold to U.S. citizens.
1830	*May 21.* Congress passes the Indian Removal Bill, which forces Indian tribes to sign removal treaties. Under the terms of such a treaty, Indians exchange land in Michigan for land west of the Mississippi. Great Lakes Indians fight fiercely against removal. Many Indians, including Simon Pokagon's Potawatomis, nevertheless remain in Michigan. Northern Michigan Native Americans never considered removal.
1836	*March 28.* U.S. government signs Treaty of Washington with the Ottawas and Chippewas. This treaty sells (cedes) large portions of what is now northern and western Michigan and the eastern portion of Michigan's Upper Peninsula. Although the land is sold, tribes keep the right to hunt, fish, and gather on ceded lands "until the land is required for settlement." Indians also receive money, goods, certain services, and land for homes.
1837	*January 26.* Michigan becomes the twenty-sixth state in the Union.
1842	*October 4.* U.S. government signs Treaty of LaPointe with the Chippewas. This treaty sells (cedes) lands in the western part of

   © PATRICK RUSSELL LEBEAU 2005 / ALL RIGHTS RESERVED

Michigan's Upper Peninsula. Although the land is sold, tribes keep the right to hunt, fish, and gather on ceded lands "until the land is required for settlement."

1849 Indian office is transferred from War Department to newly created Interior Department.

1855 U.S. government signs Treaties of Detroit. These treaties with different Ottawa and Chippewa bands uphold the right of Michigan's Native Americans to keep their homelands within the state, arranges individual allotments, and reverses many other articles of the "removal treaties" that had been designed to take away Indian treaty rights. Thus, this treaty stops Indian removal in Michigan and provides land and money originally promised to Michigan Indians in the 1836 Treaty of Washington.

1861–65 U.S. Civil War

1862 Secretary of the Interior Caleb Smith changes Indian policy. Indians are no longer regarded as independent nations but rather as "wards of the government."

1864 *March 15.* Federal law regards Indians as competent witnesses and allows them to testify in trials involving white people.

1869 *April 10.* Congress establishes the Board of Indian Commissioners to oversee the administration of Indian affairs.

1869 *April 21.* President Ulysses S. Grant appoints Brigadier General Ely S. Parker, a Tonawanda Seneca chief, as the first Indian commissioner of Indian affairs.

1870–86 Final Indian reservations are created.

1871 *March 3.* Congress ends treaty making with Indians but also declares that existing treaties will remain in effect.

1878 U.S. government establishes Indian police forces for reservation supervision.

1881 U.S. Supreme Court rules that the federal court has no jurisdiction in a case of one Indian killing another.

1885 *March 3.* Congress passes Indian Major Crimes Act which gives federal courts jurisdiction over major criminal offenses in Indian territories and on reservations.

1886 *December 14.* New federal policy states that "no books in any Indian language must be used or instruction given in that language."

1887 *February 7.* The General (Dawes) Allotment Act calls for the breakup of tribally owned lands by dividing the total land base for individual allotments and selling surplus land.

1908 Winters Doctrine holds that the establishment of an Indian reservation implies sufficient water to enable Indians to live on the lands.

© PATRICK RUSSELL LEBEAU 2005 / ALL RIGHTS RESERVED

1924	*June 2.* Congress passes Indian Citizenship Act. In part in gratitude for Indians' contributions in World War I, in which many Indians served although they were not subject to the draft, citizenship is granted to all Indians who are not yet citizens. The act gives Indians citizenship both as members of tribes and as citizens of the United States.
1925	Clinton Rickard, a Tuscarora Indian, helps to organize the Indian Defense League. The league successfully persuades the U.S. government to restore the Jay Treaty (1794) right of Indians to pass freely back and forth between Canada and the United States.
1928	Meriam Report cites the General Allotment Act as reason for impoverished conditions on Indian lands.
1934	*June 18.* Indian Reorganization Act reverses the allotment policy, providing for tribal ownership of land and ostensibly giving elected tribal councils the power to control budgets, hire attorneys, and incorporate.
1935	Indian Arts and Crafts Board is established to protect the market in Indian arts and crafts.
1944	*November 15.* National Congress of the American Indians is formed.
1946	U.S. Congress establishes the Indian Claims Commission to settle land claims against the United States, provide financial compensation, and acquire title to millions of acres of illegally seized Indian land.
1952–57	The Bureau of Indian Affairs' "relocation program" moves 17,000 Indians from reservations to such cities as Los Angeles, Chicago, Detroit, and San Francisco.
1953	*August 1.* U.S. Congress resolves to abolish the special relationship it has with Indian tribes and Indian treaties, a new policy known as "termination."
1968	*March 6.* President Lyndon B. Johnson proposes "a goal that ends . . . 'termination' of Indian programs and stresses self-determination."
1968	*April 11.* Congress passes the American Indian Civil Rights Act, which extends the Bill of Rights to Indian people living on reservations.
1971	In *People of the State of Michigan v. William Jondreau* (Jondreau Decision), the Michigan Supreme Court recognizes the right of Keweenaw Bay Indian Community members to fish in the Keweenaw Bay waters of Lake Superior without regard to Michigan fishing regulations.

© PATRICK RUSSELL LEBEAU 2005 / ALL RIGHTS RESERVED

1974   In *U.S. v. Washington State* (Boldt decision), the U.S. district court upholds the right of tribes in the Northwest to fish and manage fisheries.

1975   *January 4.* Congress passes the Indian Self-Determination Act and Education Assistance Act, mandating that the federal government will allow Indian tribes to administer federal programs if they desire to do so.

1978   *August 11.* Congress passes the American Indian Religious Freedom Act, officially guaranteeing Indians First Amendment rights of religious freedom.

1981   In *United States v. Michigan* (Judge Fox decision), the U.S. western district court of Michigan confirms the rights of the Bay Mills, Sault Ste. Marie, and Grand Traverse Bands of Michigan Indians to fish in ceded areas of the Great Lakes based on the 1836 Treaty of Washington.

1987   *February 25.* In *California et al. v. Cabazon Band of Mission Indians et al.*, the U.S. Supreme Court upholds the right of the Cabazon Reservation to hold high-stakes bingo games. This decision paves the way for Michigan's Indian reservations to create gambling operations based on their treaty rights.

1988   *April 20.* Congress repeals the 1953 termination resolution.

1990   *October 30.* President George H. W. Bush signs into law the Native American Language Act, which reverses past policy that suppressed and exterminated Indian languages and cultures.

1990   *November 16.* Congress passes the Repatriation Act, which requires the return of Indian human remains, funerary objects, sacred objects, and objects of cultural heritage.

© PATRICK RUSSELL LEBEAU 2005 / ALL RIGHTS RESERVED

[3.3] SOVEREIGNTY OF TRIBAL GOVERNMENTS: BASIC VOCABULARY AND INTRODUCTION

Basic Vocabulary

- *Sovereignty* is supremacy of authority or rule as exercised by a sovereign or sovereign state, royal rank, authority, or power and complete independence and self-government. In addition, *sovereignty* is defined as a territory existing as an independent state (American Heritage Dictionary).
- *Exclusion* of state law from Indian-held lands means that an Indian tribe "is a distinct community, occupying its own territory, with boundaries accurately described, in which the laws of [Michigan] can have no force" (Chief Justice John Marshall, *Worcester v. Georgia* [1831]).

Introduction

The ability of Michigan's Indians to self-govern, set up gambling casinos, and have a common land base has confused many people. Why do Indians have these rights when no one else does? The answer is that Indians are not the only people with these powers. We all have them in the form of our U.S. and state governments. For example, Congress could pass a law legalizing casino gambling, and the state of Michigan has a limited legalized gambling system in the form of the lottery. The federal government owns "public land" in every state in the Union, and the state of Michigan owns land as well. Public lands belong to every U.S. citizen; state-held lands can be said to belong to the citizens of that state.

Confusion arises when we mistake the rights of individual people with the rights of governments. The U.S. government, state governments, and tribal governments are separate entities within the overall makeup of the United States of America. Each can create laws and regulate activities within its jurisdiction. The U.S. government is supreme and makes laws and regulations by which states and tribes must abide, but the U.S. government allows states and tribes a great deal of autonomy. States and tribes, however, cannot separate themselves from the U.S. government to negotiate with foreign nations, for example. The central federal government has the exclusive right to act on behalf of the nation as whole. State governments act on behalf of their citizens. Therefore, if a state wants casino gambling, the choice is up to the voters of that state. Tribal governments have similar rights, privileges, and responsibilities. Tribal

© PATRICK RUSSELL LEBEAU 2005 / ALL RIGHTS RESERVED

governments act on behalf and with the consent of tribal members. This ability and right to establish a government are key to understanding the concept of sovereignty.

So, when you think of why Indians have rights and privileges, think of governments. You have rights and privileges as both a citizen of the United States as a whole and as a citizen of your state. Some of Michigan's Indian people are citizens of the United States, the state of Michigan, and their own tribes. The sovereignty of Michigan's Indian tribes is recognized and validated by Michigan's Indian treaties.

© PATRICK RUSSELL LEBEAU 2005 / ALL RIGHTS RESERVED

① Treaties are solemn agreements between two sovereign nations and are upheld by the U.S. Constitution. Treaties are contracts. Any exchanges or promises specified within treaties must be carried out. (Study Article 6, paragraph 2, of the U.S. Constitution.)

② In exchange for their land, Michigan Indians received annuities (money), agricultural equipment, experts to help them to learn skills and professions, and schools (or schooling) to teach Indian children reading, writing, and arithmetic. The United States also agreed to protect the rights of Indian people and property.

③ Treaties "reserved [for Indians] land area." Treaties, therefore, created tribal boundaries and set up Indian reservations, which also helped to preserve their existence as a distinct people.

④ Indians reserved hunting and fishing rights, meaning that Indians held onto these particular rights: they did not exchange them for money or anything else. Consequently, Indians have a legal right to fish and hunt on ceded lands (lands sold in a treaty agreement).

⑤ Indian treaties ceded millions of acres of land to the federal government and to the state of Michigan. The government took this land and sold it to settlers, lumber companies, and others. The money gained was used to pay for the federal and state governments. Lands from Indian treaties also helped support education in Michigan.

⑥ Michigan Indians could no longer live as they once had lived. For example, by 1820, Michigan Indians turned away from subsistence hunting and gathering to intensive farming and commercial fishing. The former owners of Michigan's land also suffered poverty, loss of population, and loss of traditional lands and life.

⑦ Article 6, paragraph 2, of the U.S. Constitution is known as the Supremacy Clause. This section states that treaties are the supreme law of the land. Treaties are superior to any conflicting state law. The sovereignty of Indian people is established in Article 1, section 8, of the U.S. Constitution. Foreign nations, the states, and Indian nations are the three sources of sovereignty identified in the U.S. Constitution.

⑧ Since the first treaty was signed in 1778, hundreds of court battles have waged over the interpretation of treaties. The canons of construction have evolved as rules for interpreting treaty disputes. (1) If any confusion in interpretation of articles or intent of articles in treaties arises, they must be interpreted to favor Indians. (2) Because treaties were negotiated and written in English, treaties must be interpreted as the Indians would have understood them.

 © **PATRICK RUSSELL LEBEAU 2005 / ALL RIGHTS RESERVED**

[3.5] INDIANS TREATIES AS SUPREME LAW OF THE LAND: BASIC VOCABULARY, INTRODUCTION, AND MAJOR COURT CASES AND DECISIONS

Basic Vocabulary

- A *treaty* is a formal agreement between two or more countries or sovereign governments.

Article 6, paragraph 2, of the of the U.S. Constitution states, "This constitution, and the laws of the United States which shall be made in pursuance thereof; and all treaties made, or which shall be made, under authority of the United States shall be the Supreme law of the land; and the judges in every state shall be bound thereby, anything in the constitution or laws of any state to the contrary notwithstanding."

Introduction

Treaties are artifacts of the past, primary sources for the historical exploration of Indian history. However, treaties are also living documents. Treaties are as valid today as the day the signatures at the bottom of each treaty first dried. You can compare this to how the U.S. Constitution is just as valid and relevant to Americans living today as it was to those Americans living in 1789. The Constitution defines our way of life, establishes our governmental system, and grants and protects our rights and privileges as U.S. citizens. Likewise, Indian treaties define Indians as a self-governing, land-based people with special rights and privileges. Treaties are also protected and enforced by our Constitution under Article 6, paragraph 2, which states that treaties are the "Supreme law of the land."

Major Court Cases and Decisions

1971   In *People of the State of Michigan v. William Jondreau* (Jondreau decision), the Michigan Supreme Court recognizes the right of the Keweenaw Bay Indian Community members to fish in the Keweenaw Bay waters of Lake Superior without regard to Michigan fishing regulations.

© PATRICK RUSSELL LEBEAU 2005 / ALL RIGHTS RESERVED

1974   In *U.S. v. Washington State* (Boldt decision) the U.S. district court upholds the right of tribes in the Northwest to fish and to manage fisheries.

1981   In *U.S. v. Michigan* (Judge Fox decision), the U.S. district court confirms the rights of the Bay Mills, Sault Ste. Marie, and Grand Traverse Bands of Michigan Chippewa to fish in ceded areas of the Great Lakes based on the 1836 Treaty of Washington.

1987   In *California et al. v. Cabazon Band of Mission Indians et al.*, the U.S. Supreme Court upholds the right of the Cabazon Reservation to hold high-stakes bingo games. This decision paves the way for Michigan's Indian reservations to create gambling operations based on their treaty rights.

    © PATRICK RUSSELL LEBEAU 2005 / ALL RIGHTS RESERVED

1807   *November 17.* U.S. government signs Treaty of Detroit with the
        Ottawas, Chippewas, Wyandots, and Potawatomis. This treaty sells
        (cedes) large portions of what is now southeastern Michigan.
        Although the land is sold, tribes keep the right to hunt, fish, and
        gather on ceded lands "until the land is required for settlement."

1819   *September 24.* U.S. government signs Treaty of Saginaw with the
        Chippewas. This treaty sells (cedes) large portions of what is now
        the middle part of Michigan's Lower Peninsula. Although the land is
        sold, tribes keep the right to hunt, fish, and gather on ceded lands
        "until the land is required for settlement."

1821   *August 29.* U.S. government signs Treaty of Chicago with the
        Chippewas, the Ottawas, and the Potawatomis. This treaty sells
        (cedes) large portions of what is now the southwestern Lower
        Peninsula. Although the land is sold, tribes keep the right to hunt,
        fish, and gather on ceded lands until sold to U.S citizens.

1828   *September 20.* U.S. government signs treaty with the Potawatomis
        that sells (cedes) land in extreme southwestern Michigan. Although
        the land is sold, tribes keep the right to hunt, fish, and gather on
        ceded lands until sold to U.S. citizens.

1836   *March 28.* U.S. government signs Treaty of Washington with the
        Ottawas and Chippewas. This treaty sells (cedes) large portions of
        what is now northern Michigan and the eastern portion of Michigan's
        Upper Peninsula. Although the land is sold, tribes keep the right to
        hunt, fish, and gather on ceded lands. Indians also receive money,
        goods, certain services, and lands for homes. This meant that reserva-
        tions were to be created. Instead, Congress tried to change what was
        promised in the treaty and forcibly remove Indians to lands west of
        the Mississippi under the 1830 Indian Removal Bill.

1837   *January 26.* As a direct result of the above treaties, Michigan
        becomes the twenty-sixth state in the Union.

1842   *October 4.* U.S. government signs Treaty of LaPointe with the
        Chippewas. This treaty sells (cedes) lands in the western part of
        Michigan's Upper Peninsula. Although the land is sold, tribes keep
        the right to hunt, fish, and gather on ceded lands "until the land is
        required for settlement."

© PATRICK RUSSELL LEBEAU 2005 / ALL RIGHTS RESERVED

1855   U.S. government signs Treaty of Detroit with the Ottawa and
        Chippewa, July 31, and Chippewa, August 2. This treaty upholds the
        right of Michigan's Indians to keep their homelands within the state
        and reverses many other articles of the "removal treaties" that had
        been designed to take away Indian treaty rights. Thus, this treaty stops
        Indian removal in Michigan and provides land and money originally
        promised to Michigan Indians in the 1836 Treaty of Washington.

 © PATRICK RUSSELL LEBEAU 2005 / ALL RIGHTS RESERVED

[3.7] NEGOTIATING AN INDIAN TREATY: TEACHER MASTER

General Instructions for Interpreters

You are to convey each party's desires and proposals to the other party. They are not allowed to speak directly to one another. Try your best to be accurate. You also determine when the negotiations are over. You help write out the treaty. You can either use the mock treaty provided or use the mock treaty as a pattern for writing your own.

General Instructions for U.S. Government Officials

Your goal is to get the Indians to sign the treaty. You are open to most proposals that do not cost a lot of money. You also realize that these Indian people need at least some land. You can negotiate how much, although your goal is to get as much of the land as possible. Confine the Indians to the space (the part of the classroom) you have set aside for them. You should agree to anything that does not cost money. You want to pay some money for the land you are getting. You have a budget of $1 million. However, you want to spend this money on items and services that will "civilize" the Indian people rather than giving out cash. You also help the interpreters draft the treaty and make sure everyone signs.

General Instructions for Supreme Court Justices

Review the challengers' paper and the Indians' response. Based on your understanding of treaties, the articles relevant to treaties in the Constitution, and the canons of construction, decide who you think is right and write out an explanation of why you reached that decision.

General Instructions for Indian Tribe

Most of the Indian land base will be taken away from you whether you like it or not. Your goal is to get something in exchange for that land without a heated confrontation. You want: (1) some land set aside for your permanent use and guaranteed to be yours forever; (2) hunting, fishing, and gathering rights so that your people will have food; and (3) guarantees that the government will pro-

© PATRICK RUSSELL LEBEAU 2005 / ALL RIGHTS RESERVED

vide for the education of your children and their descendants. You should also create pictographs (small drawings of animals, objects found in nature, or anything else you can imagine); these will be your signatures. You must also draft a response to the challengers and submit it to the Supreme Court. Your response must include the reasons you think they are wrong.

General Instructions for Challengers

You move into the areas of the classroom not occupied by Indians. After the treaty is signed, you decide on one article (or part of the treaty) that you will dispute. You must compose a short paper identifying the article and explaining why you do not like it. Submit your paper to the Supreme Court.

© PATRICK RUSSELL LEBEAU 2005 / ALL RIGHTS RESERVED

[3.8] NEGOTIATING AN INDIAN TREATY: INTERPRETERS

Y ou are to convey each party's desires and proposals to the other party. They are not allowed to speak directly to one another. Try your best to be accurate. You also determine when the negotiations are over. You help write out the treaty. You can either use the mock treaty provided or use the mock treaty as a pattern for writing your own.

Basic Vocabulary

- *Ceded territory* refers to specific lands or territories sold in treaties. Treaty rights to hunt, fish, and gather can be exercised in the ceded territory under tribal regulation.

- *Plenary power* means that only the federal government can negotiate with Indian nations. Individuals and state (or other local) governments cannot directly negotiate with Indians. The federal government is responsible for creating legislation affecting Indian affairs. However, these negotiations and laws must not violate the U.S. Constitution.

- *Reservation* is the land owned by an Indian tribe and is now considered the tribe's homeland. This land is often described and reserved in treaties.

- *Reserved rights* means that Indians have the full right and power to self-govern, to hold land in common on "reserved lands," and to hunt, gather, and fish on ceded lands.

- *Sovereignty* is supremacy of authority or rule as exercised by a sovereign or sovereign state, royal rank, authority, or power as well as complete independence and self-government. In addition, *sovereignty* is defined as a territory existing as an independent state (American Heritage Dictionary).

- *Treaty* is a formal agreement between two or more countries or sovereign governments.

- *Trust relationship* means that the federal government must protect Indian tribes in the same manner that parents protect and look out for the welfare and safety of their children.

© PATRICK RUSSELL LEBEAU 2005 / ALL RIGHTS RESERVED

[3.9] NEGOTIATING AN INDIAN TREATY: U.S. GOVERNMENT OFFICIALS

Your goal is to get the Indians to sign the treaty. You are open to most proposals that do not cost a lot of money. You also realize that these Indian people need at least some land. You can negotiate how much, although your goal is to get as much of the land as possible. Confine the Indians to the space (the part of the classroom) you have set aside for them. You should agree to anything that does not cost money. You want to pay some money for the land you are getting. You have a budget of $1 million. However, you want to spend this money on items and services that will "civilize" the Indian people rather than giving out cash. You also help the interpreters draft the treaty and make sure everyone signs.

Basic Vocabulary

- *Ceded territory* refers to specific lands or territories sold in treaties. Treaty rights to hunt, fish, and gather can be exercised in the ceded territory under tribal regulation.
- *Plenary power* means that only the federal government can negotiate with Indian nations. Individuals and state (or other local) governments cannot directly negotiate with Indians. The federal government is responsible for creating legislation affecting Indian affairs. However, these negotiations and laws must not violate the U.S. Constitution.
- *Reserved rights* means that Indians have the full right and power to self-govern, to hold land in common on "reserved lands," and to hunt, gather, and fish on ceded lands.
- *Sovereignty* is supremacy of authority or rule as exercised by a sovereign or sovereign state, royal rank, authority, or power as well as complete independence and self-government. In addition, *sovereignty* is defined as a territory existing as an independent state (American Heritage Dictionary).
- *Treaty* is a formal agreement between two or more countries or sovereign governments.
- *Trust relationship* means that the federal government must protect Indian tribes in the same manner that parents protect and look out for the welfare and safety of their children.

© PATRICK RUSSELL LEBEAU 2005 / ALL RIGHTS RESERVED

[3.10] NEGOTIATING AN INDIAN TREATY: SUPREME COURT JUSTICES

Review the challengers' paper and the Indians' response. Based on your understanding of treaties, the articles relevant to treaties in the Constitution, and the canons of construction, decide who you think is right and write out an explanation of why you reached that decision.

Basic Vocabulary

- *Article 1, section 8* of the U.S. Constitution grants Congress the power "to regulate commerce with foreign nations, and among the several States, and with Indian tribes."
- *Article 6, paragraph 2*, of the of the U.S. Constitution states, "This constitution, and the laws of the United States which shall be made in pursuance thereof; and all treaties made, or which shall be made, under authority of the United States shall be the Supreme law of the land; and the judges in every state shall be bound thereby, anything in the constitution or laws of any state to the contrary notwithstanding."

Worcester v. Georgia

In *Worcester v. Georgia* (1831), Chief Justice John Marshall defined the relationship between Indian nations and the U.S. and state governments. This relationship is explained by the following terms:

- *Plenary power* means that only the federal government can negotiate with Indian nations. Individuals and state (or other local) governments cannot directly negotiate with Indians. The federal government is responsible for creating legislation affecting Indian affairs. However, these negotiations and laws must not violate the U.S. Constitution.
- *Trust relationship* means that the federal government must protect Indian tribes in the same manner that parents protect and look out for the welfare and safety of their children.
- *Reserved rights* means that Indians have the full right and power to self-govern, to hold land in common on "reserved lands," and to hunt, gather, and fish on ceded lands.

© PATRICK RUSSELL LEBEAU 2005 / ALL RIGHTS RESERVED

- *Exclusion* of state law from Indian-held lands means that an Indian tribe "is a distinct community, occupying its own territory, with boundaries accurately described, in which the laws of [Michigan] can have no force."

The Canons of Construction

The canons of construction establish two important rules of interpretation:

1. If any confusion in interpretation of articles or intent of articles in treaties arises, they must be interpreted to favor Indians.
2. Because treaties were negotiated and written in English, a language Indians did not understand, treaties must be interpreted as the Indians would have understood them.

© PATRICK RUSSELL LEBEAU 2005 / ALL RIGHTS RESERVED

[3.11] NEGOTIATING AN INDIAN TREATY: INDIAN TRIBE

Most of the Indian land base will be taken away from you whether you like it or not. Your goal is to get something in exchange for that land without a heated confrontation. You want: (1) some land set aside for your permanent use and guaranteed to be yours forever; (2) hunting, fishing, and gathering rights so that your people will have food; and (3) guarantees that the government will provide for the education of your children and their descendants. You should also create pictographs (small drawings of animals, objects found in nature, or anything else you can imagine); these will be your signatures. You must also draft a response to the challengers and submit it to the Supreme Court. Your response must include the reasons you think they are wrong.

Basic Vocabulary

- *Ceded territory* refers to specific lands or territories sold in treaties. Treaty rights to hunt, fish, and gather can be exercised in the ceded territory under tribal regulation.
- *Reservation* is the land owned by an Indian tribe and is now considered the tribe's homeland. This land is often described and reserved in treaties.
- *Reserved rights* means that Indians have the full right and power to self-govern, to hold land in common on "reserved lands," and to hunt, gather, and fish on ceded lands.
- *Sovereignty* is supremacy of authority or rule as exercised by a sovereign or sovereign state, royal rank, authority, or power as well as complete independence and self-government. In addition, *sovereignty* is defined as a territory existing as an independent state (American Heritage Dictionary).
- *Promises, goods, services, and money* are what government officials have to pay for Indian land.
- *Treaty* is a formal agreement between two or more countries or sovereign governments.

© PATRICK RUSSELL LEBEAU 2005 / ALL RIGHTS RESERVED

[3.12] NEGOTIATING AN INDIAN TREATY: CHALLENGERS

You move into the areas of the classroom not occupied by Indians. After the treaty is signed, you decide on one article (or part of the treaty) that you will dispute. You must compose a short paper identifying the article and explaining why you do not like it. Submit your paper to the Supreme Court.

Basic Vocabulary

- *Ceded territory* refers to specific lands or territories sold in treaties. Treaty rights to hunt, fish, and gather can be exercised in the ceded territory under tribal regulation.
- *Exclusion* of state law from Indian-held lands means that an Indian tribe "is a distinct community, occupying its own territory, with boundaries accurately described, in which the laws of [Michigan] can have no force" (Chief Justice John Marshall, *Worcester v. Georgia* [1831]).
- *Plenary power* means that only the federal government can negotiate with Indian nations. Individuals and state (or other local) governments cannot directly negotiate with Indians. The federal government is responsible for creating legislation affecting Indian affairs. However, these negotiations and laws must not violate the U.S. Constitution.
- *Reservation* is the land owned by an Indian tribe and is now considered the tribe's homeland. This land is often described and reserved in treaties.
- *Reserved rights* means that Indians have the full right and power to self-govern, to hold land in common on "reserved lands," and to hunt, gather, and fish on ceded lands.
- *Sovereignty* is supremacy of authority or rule as exercised by a sovereign or sovereign state, royal rank, authority, or power as well as complete independence and self-government. In addition, *sovereignty* is defined as a territory existing as an independent state (American Heritage Dictionary).
- *Treaty* is a formal agreement between two or more countries or sovereign governments.
- *Trust relationship* means that the federal government must protect Indian tribes in the same manner that parents protect and look out for the welfare and safety of their children.

© PATRICK RUSSELL LEBEAU 2005 / ALL RIGHTS RESERVED

[3.13] TREATY WITH THE INDIAN PEOPLE OF _____ CLASS

Articles of the Treaty Made and Concluded at _____ in the Territory of Michigan on the _____ Day of _____ .

Article the First

The peace and friendship between the United States and the _____ shall be perpetual.

Article the Second

The said _____ do hereby cede and relinquish all their lands and territory of Michigan, except for those lands set aside for their specific use. Indians may also hunt and fish on all public lands.

Article the Third

In further and full consideration of said land cession, the United States agrees to pay lots of money: for living expenses; to build schools, mills, blacksmith shops, farms, and fences; for breaking lands; and for educational purposes, agricultural improvements, and civilization. More money will be given to said tribe for many years to come.

Article the Fourth

Rules and regulations to protect the rights of persons and property among the Indian parties to the treaty may be prescribed and enforced as the president or the Congress of the United States shall direct.

In witness whereof the said made of Indian People of _____ and _____ commissioners of the part of the United States have hereunto set their hands at _____ this day of _____ (Sign below)

© PATRICK RUSSELL LEBEAU 2005 / ALL RIGHTS RESERVED

① The 1836 Treaty of Washington between the United States and the Ottawas and Chippewas and the 1855 Treaty at Detroit between the Ottawa, Chippewa, and Saginaw Chippewa included provisions for Indian education. The State of Michigan was established in 1837.

② Indian education was the responsibility of the Bureau of Indian Affairs (BIA) of the federal government.

③ Mission boarding schools, day schools, and public schools (before 1888) all failed as methods of educating Native American children.

④ Manual labor training (MLT) schools were established in the state of Michigan between 1888 and 1893. These schools provided technical training for Native American youth.

⑤ These MLT schools were closed in the 1930s. The land and buildings were given to the state of Michigan in exchange for educating Michigan's Indians as promised and stipulated in U.S. treaties made with the same Indians.

⑥ The state of Michigan did not honor this promise until 1976, when Native Americans fought for and won the right to free public education, including college tuition at state-supported institutions. As of this writing, Native American people who can prove Indian blood quantum, according to federal guidelines, can attend Michigan's public institutions of higher learning tuition-free.

 © PATRICK RUSSELL LEBEAU 2005 / ALL RIGHTS RESERVED

[3.15] TREATY WITH THE OTTAWA AND CHIPPEWA, MARCH 28, 1836

Articles of a treaty made and concluded at the city of Washington in the District of Columbia, between Henry Schoolcraft, commissioner on the part of the United States, and the Ottawa and Chippewa nations of Indians, by their chiefs and delegates.[In the 1855 treaty, the "nations" were dissolved.]

Article First

[Designation of boundary lines ceded to the United States]

Article Second

From the cession aforesaid the tribes reserve for their own use, to hold in common the following tracts for the term of five years from the date of ratification of this treaty and no longer; unless the United States shall grant them permission to remain on said lands for a longer period, namely: One tract of fifty thousand acres to be located on Little Traverse bay: one tract of twenty thousand acres to be located on the north shore of Grand Traverse bay: one tract of seventy thousand acres to be located on, or north of the Pierie Marquetta river [*sic*], one tract of one thousand acres to be located by Mujeekewis, on Thunder-bay river.

Article Third

There shall also be reserved for the use of the Chippewas living north of the straits of Michilimackinac, the following tracts for the term of five years from the date of ratification of this treaty, and no longer, unless the United States shall grant them permission to remain on said lands for a longer period of time, that is to say: Two tracts of three miles square each, on the north shores of the said straits, between Point-au-Barbe and Mille Coquin river, including the fishing grounds in front of such reservations, to be located by a council of chiefs. The Beaver islands of Lake Michigan for the use the Beaver-island Indians. Round island, opposite Michilimackinac, as a place of encampment for the Indians, to be under charge of the Indian department. The islands of the Chenos, with a part of the adjacent north coast of Lake Huron, corresponding in length, and one mile in depth, Sugar Island, with its islets, in the river of St.

© PATRICK RUSSELL LEBEAU 2005 / ALL RIGHTS RESERVED

Mary's. Six hundred and forty acres, at the mission of the Little Rapids. A tract commencing at the mouth of the Pississowining [This name was invented by Henry Schoolcraft] river, south of Point Iroquois, thence across the portage to the Tacquimenon river, and down the same to its mouth, including the small islands and fishing grounds, in front of this reservation. Six hundred and forty acres, on Grand Island, and two thousand acres, on the main land south of it. Two sections on the northern extremity of Green Bay, to be located by council of chiefs. All locations, left indefinite by this, and preceding articles, shall be made by the proper chiefs, under the direction of the President. It is understood that the reservation for a place of fishing and encampment, made under the treaty of St. Mary's of the 16th of June 1820, remain unaffected by this treaty.

Article Fourth

In consideration of the foregoing cessions, the United States engage to pay to the Ottawa and Chippewa nations, the following sums, namely: [lots of money]. . . .

© PATRICK RUSSELL LEBEAU 2005 / ALL RIGHTS RESERVED

[3.16] QUESTIONS FOR THOUGHT AND DISCUSSION
▶ LESSON THE THIRD

Part 1 ▶ Sovereignty of Tribal Governments

Activity A: The Meaning of Sovereignty: Article 1, Section 8, U.S. Constitution

① What are treaties? How can a treaty be proof that Indian tribes have (or possess) sovereignty?

② Read Article 1, section 8, of the U.S. Constitution. This is the accepted source establishing the sovereignty of Indian tribes. Write a paragraph explaining the context into which Indian tribes are put. Is the conjunction *and* important?

Activity B: Sovereignty, Government, and Jurisdiction

① A government of a nation or state is necessary for a sovereignty to exist. Why?

② For the most part, a land base, with borders, is necessary to exercise jurisdiction. Why?

③ The U.S. government has jurisdiction over every person and government within the borders of the United States but not for the most part over any person or government outside its borders. The same can be said for states. Explain why this is also true for Indian tribes.

④ If Indian tribes have land bases and governments within the boundaries of states, why cannot states exercise state jurisdiction over Indian tribes?

Activity C: Exploring the Treaty Rights and the U.S. Constitution Timeline

① Identify acts, cases, bills, or other declarations that demonstrate, affirm, or provide examples of Indian sovereignty. How do Indian tribes exercise the power of self-government?

② In what cases was Indian sovereignty challenged?

③ Summarize what you have learned.

© PATRICK RUSSELL LEBEAU 2005 / ALL RIGHTS RESERVED

Activity A: The Supreme Law of the Land

1. What does the "supreme law of the land" mean?
2. Can anyone break this law? Amend this law?
3. How does the "supreme law of the land" validate the special rights and privileges of Indian tribes and people?

Activity B: Exploring the Treaty Rights and the U.S. Constitution Timeline

1. Identify acts, cases, bills, or other declarations that demonstrate, affirm, or provide examples of how treaties are the "supreme law of the land."
2. The state of Michigan and some individuals have challenged the legal force of Indian treaties. Find those cases on the timeline (or on the Internet or in newspaper articles) and write a short paragraph explaining why the Supreme Court was compelled to uphold the rights of Indian tribes.

Part 3 ▶ Negotiating an Indian Treaty

Activity A: Role-Playing Treaty Negotiations

1. What problems did you encounter or witness as the two parties tried to negotiate and sign a treaty?
2. Do the interpreters get in the way? Could you have accomplished your task more easily without them?
3. No matter what the Indians negotiate for, why do they still lose out?
4. Who do the challengers represent in real life? Why might they have some grievance or dispute with the Indian treaty?
5. Do the Supreme Court justices have to decide in favor of the Indians? Why or why not?
6. How do you make promises? Do you keep them? Are you obligated to honor them? Is a moral code part of the idea behind making promises?
7. If you make a promise in writing and sign your name to that written promise, is the promise more important? Does your signature add validity to your promise?

 © PATRICK RUSSELL LEBEAU 2005 / ALL RIGHTS RESERVED

Activity B: Exploring "Treaty with the Indian People of _____ Class"

1. Article the First: What does this article mean? How do you define the words *peace, friendship,* and *perpetual?*

2. Article the Second: What do Indians get in return for "ceding and relinquishing" all their land? Do they in fact "give" away "all" of their land?

3. Article the Third: This is the payment clause. Is money the only currency of exchange? Money is stipulated to buy goods and services. What is the nature of these goods and services? How do they help Indian people? What are they designed to accomplish?

4. Article the Fourth: Why does the U.S. government want to "protect the rights" of Indian people? What does *protect* mean? Why is it important? Does this mean that the U.S. government can harm or fully control the rights of Indian people?

Activity C: Four Concepts Inherent in Indian Treaties

1. Which concept makes casino gambling possible?
2. The Michigan Indian Education is justified by which category?
3. Which concept allows for commercial fishing by recognized tribal members?
4. Why did federal courts reverse restrictions and prohibitions against Indian fishing and gambling operations?

Part 4 ▶ Treaty Rights Lost and Won Back

Activity A: Indian Education as a Specific Compensation for Ceded Land:

The Michigan Indian Tuition Waiver Act ("Indian Treaties: Michigan Indian Education")

1. Explain in your own words why Native Americans get "free" tuition. Is the tuition "free"? Is this fair? Explain why or why not.

2. Should this promise to provide for the education of Michigan's Indians been honored before 1976? Why or why not?

3. Why would education be important to Native American people?

© PATRICK RUSSELL LEBEAU 2005 / ALL RIGHTS RESERVED

Activity B: Fishing Rights

1. Based on the information provided to you and on the "Treaty Rights and the U.S. Constitution Timeline," why do Michigan's Indians to this day have a right to fish on ceded lands?

2. Why would the Indian signers of the treaties want to keep fishing and hunting and gathering (of wild rice, berries, or maple syrup, for example) as a reserved right? What purpose would it serve?

3. Studying your answer to question 2, you have probably came up with several practical reasons why Indian people would want to fish, hunt, and gather. But that was in the past. Can you come up with practical reasons for hunting and fishing and gathering in Michigan today? Are they the same as or different from your answers to question 2? Explain. Can you contemplate any modern reasons to fish? If so, explain.

Activity C: Casino Gambling: An Act of Self-Government Derived from Tribal Sovereignty, Self-Determination, and Jurisdiction

1. Study the "Treaty Rights and the U.S. Constitution Timeline." What legislation supports the concept of self-determination and self-government as applied to the Indian tribes of Michigan?

2. Why do (or why can) Indian tribes have governments? Is a land base important for this ability to self-govern? Explain.

3. Casino gambling is arguably not a traditional activity of Indian tribes. Why is this an invalid argument for restricting Indian tribes' ability to operate casinos?

4. How are treaties involved in establishing the right of Indian tribes to set up casino gambling on their tribal lands?

Part 5 ▶ Indian Treaties: Exploring a Real Treaty

Activity A: Exploring a Real Treaty

1. Where does the treaty set aside land for Ottawas and Chippewas? Can you figure out where in the state of Michigan these lands are located? Is this land held in common?

2. Where does the treaty discuss hunting and fishing rights? What does the phrase "until the land is required for settlement" mean to you? What if the land is never required for settlement?

 © PATRICK RUSSELL LEBEAU 2005 / ALL RIGHTS RESERVED

③ Is any money given out? If so, to whom? Why?

④ Explain in your own words what other provisions this treaty includes. Explain the meaning of *improvements*. Why do the Indians need blacksmiths or gunsmiths?

© PATRICK RUSSELL LEBEAU 2005 / ALL RIGHTS RESERVED

LESSON THE FOURTH

How Historical Maps Influence
Thinking about Michigan's Indians

MAJOR PREMISE

With a few specific exceptions, like Helen Hornbeck Tanner's *The Atlas of Great Lakes Indian History*, most historical and contemporary maps tell a story of U.S. history and state building that overlooks reserved rights and original landownership by Michigan's Indians.

OBJECTIVES

To demonstrate that:

- Maps are informational: They tell us where Indians lived and live.
- Maps show possession and appropriation of land and property.
- Maps show Michigan Indian treaties as land-acquisition instruments and state-building documents.
- Although few designated reservations were actually surveyed and in some cases substitutions were made, maps show lands reserved for Indian use in the state of Michigan.
- Maps show more about U.S. and Michigan history than about Michigan Indian history.
- Stories (personal, family, community, and cultural) can also map boundaries, affinities, and sacredness of land and environment from an Indian perspective.
- Memories and storytelling graphically reproduced can show what is important to individuals about their neighborhoods or personal activities within a fixed period of time.

Lesson the Fourth explores historical maps and their influence on the way we think about the role and place of Native Americans in U.S. and Michigan history. Besides the everyday practical use we make of maps—for example, to locate places or buildings and to offer guidance when we travel—historical maps can tell us where people lived, demonstrate why a river was important for trade, and show how the United States expanded its land base. In most U.S. history books, maps are designed to teach about the ever-changing nature of Euro-American patterns of settlement and expansion, and such maps tell very little about Native American people or cultures. Instead, a line is drawn between what is understood to be Indian land, or the "wilderness," and Euro-American land, or "civilization." Such lines are commonplace and are often formalized in governmental statutes and legislative acts such as the Proclamation Line of 1763. For Michigan Indians, the Treaty of Fort Stanwix, 1768, was most important because the treaty established the Ohio River as the boundary between U.S. and Indian lands until 1794. As lines, in the form of borders or boundaries, are depicted on historical maps, the visual image of Euro-American possession and appropriation of Indian lands of North America is made clear.

U.S. history is often taught with help of historical maps. History and social studies teachers use maps to accurately depict the surface of the earth. In the context of U.S. history, maps show the changing nature of Euro-American human-created features, such as routes, boundaries, and settlements, a history with a distinctive east-to-west axis and pattern. The historical emphasis and interest is on the activities of Euro-Americans. Native Americans are visually placed outside the boundaries of "Western civilization." The visual information conveyed in maps literally places Native Americans outside of what was "found" by explorers and later "created" by settlers. For U.S. historians and history teachers, maps help to foster students' understanding of European settlement, colonization, and western expansion; these maps are hallmarks of American history textbooks.

Although maps have many functions, most historians—as close scrutiny of the maps found in U.S. history books will corroborate—believe an undisputed function of historical maps is to show (and to claim) possession of land and to create a visual memory of natural geographic and human-created features. As primary sources, the maps created by explorers such as Christopher Columbus or commissioned surveyors like George Washington laid claim to land. When maps were produced and published for government or public examination, European possession of Indian land had official sanction. Therefore, Euro-American claims to and possession of Indian land happened long before treaties were signed with the recognized owners of the land and long before any significant Euro-American settlement of these places took place. Beyond providing the maps' informational content (identification of geographical features), these explorers' and surveyors' most important mission was to demarcate land and to lay claim to it by establishing clear-cut boundaries and visually representing these claims on maps.

Maps visually represent the natural geographic environment, and this imagery establishes a frame of reference in which students and historians can understand historical developments. For example, after learning where the Allegheny Mountains, the Great Lakes, and the Mississippi River are located, students begin to understand the nature of early colonial settlement prior to and during the Revolutionary War period and the nature of French, Spanish, and English land claims. U.S. history textbooks use heavy black (and/or color-coded) lines to demarcate the boundaries of early French and British colonial settlements. Historical maps can show how the original thirteen colonies had northern and southern boundaries and open-ended western boundaries, depicting the colonies' coast-to-coast charters. In maps depicting the latter 1700s, the often color-coded province of Quebec and territory of Louisiana visually show barriers to American expansion based on French and English land claims. These kinds of historical maps imply that Native Americans live in "unsettled lands" but do not always visually depict Indians.

U.S. maps found in history textbooks usually follow this pattern and also give a very strong impression of U.S. expansion as a process of conquering Indian people, acquiring Indian land, and then creating new states for the Union. After the American Revolution, the Ordinance of 1784 and the Northwest Ordinance of 1787 put an end to coast-to-coast charters, creating western borders for the original thirteen colonies and delineating a process for creating new states in the western territories. On U.S. history maps circa 1787, the new nation is bounded by the Mississippi River to the west, the Great Lakes to the north, and Spanish Florida to the south and is divided by the Ohio River. From such maps' perspectives, the fledgling United States is poised for expansion and the creation of new states—Ohio, Indiana, Illinois, Michigan, and Wisconsin—from the lands possessed and appropriated by a solid black line, the boundary of what was then called the Northwest Territory, even though the U.S. had to fight until 1794 to gain this objective.

After being bounded and claimed, lands such as the Northwest Territory are ripe for controlled settlement when the Native American populations are subdued and their land acquired through treaties. Resistance persisted. The Ottawas of Northern Michigan, for example, did not acknowledge the President of the U.S. as "father" (i.e., superior) rather than "brother" (i.e., equal) until 1855. But before the Northwest Territory could be incorporated into the United States, Native American title to the land had to be extinguished. Extinguishing title was much easier when Native American populations were no longer a military threat. In the Great Lakes area and especially in Michigan, removing the threat took some time. Military operations against the Native Americans of Michigan are well documented in such works as Wiley Sword's *George Washington's Indian War* and the many biographies of Pontiac and Tecumseh. For many years, the Northwest Territory was a military zone from the perspective of the U.S. military, the U.S. federal government, and European powers such as Great Britain. (See map 14 in Helen Hornbeck Tanner's *Atlas of Great Lakes Indian History* [1987] for a detailed representation of military operations in the Northwest Territory, 1774–94 and also the battle maps of the War of 1812.) Graphically, this process is depicted on historical maps in the form of symbols: tiny black squares for forts (for example, Forts Detroit, St. Joseph, and Michilimackinac) or crossed swords for battles (for example, Fallen Timbers, River Raisin, and the Siege of Detroit during the War of 1812).

Symbolic devices on maps to depict military presence serve three important functions. First, maps show that the military threat and power of Native American tribes is monitored and controlled. Second, the garrisoning of the frontier prevented claims and disputes by foreign powers and established a physical and symbolic presence, legitimizing U.S. land claims by possession. Third, an orderly settlement of lands can be shown to take place under the auspices of the federal government.

Within this framework, Michigan Indian land cessions through the treaty-making process could take place. Completing the state of Michigan in its present boundaries required the negotiation and signing of nine treaties with the tribes of Michigan. "Major American Indian Land Cessions by Treaty, with County Borders" (4.29) shows the nine treaties in a color-coded fashion: Treaty of Detroit, 1807; Treaty of Maumee, 1817; Treaty of Saginaw, 1819; Treaty of Chicago, 1821; Treaty of Carey Mission, 1828; Treaty of Chicago, 1833; Treaty of Washington, 1836; Treaty of Cedar Point, 1836; and the Treaty of LaPointe, 1842. These maps show Michigan Indian treaties as land-acquisition instruments and state-building documents.

Treaty maps also show the location of "reserved" lands, enabling the inference of the "reserved rights" stipulated in treaties. For example, many of the maps in the appended resources can be used to learn about the historical and present locations of Michigan's Native Americans and Indian reservations. Henry Schoolcraft's 1837 map of Michigan (4.2)—although controversial, exaggerated, and distorted—shows the locations and relative size of Michigan's Indian reservations. His map is included to show that the possession of Indian land is more important than the accuracy of the data and visual display of reservations. His map is a testament to the visual power of appropriation and state building via the symbolism inherent in historical maps, even though it does not agree with the data and representations depicted in maps produced after 1850. For some historians, his map is terribly inaccurate because it was created before surveyors worked north of the Grand River. Schoolcraft (1789–1865) spent most of his life in Michigan as a government agent to the Chippewas of Sault Ste. Marie and Mackinaw. As acting superintendent of Michigan in 1837, when Michigan achieved statehood, he was commissioned to delineate the boundaries of Indian reservations based on Michigan's Indian treaties. His map also included the names of the tribes involved in the treaty and their estimated populations. In the "Map of Michigan Indian Reservations" (February 16, 1996), prepared by the Michigan Department of Management and Budget, the locations of these reservations are the same, although the land base of each reservation is noticeably smaller and some of the reservations do not appear at all. (This map is available at *http://www.edwards1.com/rose/ native/indian-map.htm*). In "American Indian and Other Casinos" (4.5), images of slot machines are used as symbols of tribal sovereignty, and their placement on the map corresponds to tribal locations depicted on the Schoolcraft and 1996 maps.

Native American relationships to the environment also are easily inferred from maps. Historical dependence on hunting and fishing reveals itself when the placement of Indian reservations is studied. For the most part, reservations are close to if not identical to ancestral preferences for village locations. Most of Michigan's Indian reservations are near waterways, hunting and fishing grounds, sugar maples, and land capable of growing corn, beans, and squash. The historical reliance on fishing is reflected in the present-day tribal commercial fishing operations. The building of casinos and the tertiary infrastructure (hotels, gas stations, and convenience stores) show Native American adaptation and the impact of technological innovations on the changing nature of life on Indian reservations.

"Indian Trails in Michigan, 1763" (4.18), combined with the knowledge of how Native Americans used waterways as avenues of transportation, demonstrates the fluent movement and interaction of Michigan's Native Americans. These movements in turn show subsistence patterns, trade routes, and each tribe's relations to neighboring Native American and non–Native American communities. "Waterways, Highways, and Byways" (4.21), reveals how modern highways closely follow historical trails, rivers, and coastlines.

Indian reservations also delineate political and cultural regions. The boundaries of Indian reservations on maps illustrate the historical separation and segregation of Native Americans on lands and with their own governments. Within those boundaries, Native Americans practice politics and exercise sovereignty by electing tribal councils and chairpersons and by engaging in tribal enterprises and ventures such as building casinos and developing commercial fisheries. They celebrate tribal culture with annual powwows and with numerous ceremonial and social events. Reservations organize the political, cultural, and social characteristics of the Native American people under the commonalities of tribal identity and reservation borders.

In this lesson, the exploration of Michigan maps as they relate to Michigan's Native American populations and tribal governments and land base will help students understand the geographical significance of Michigan Indian history. With these historical and geographical perspectives, students will begin to understand how Native Americans fit into Michigan's history, society, and culture.

Shifting the perspective to the obvious question of geographic education, several maps depicting the state of Michigan will be compared to maps created and rendered through narrative accounts and symbolic devices of personal invention. For example, many of the following questions will be explored: How would a Potawatomi create a map of trails and treaties? How would you map your morning? How can a story be a map? Do stories of places, towns, and family homes or farms resemble the stories of Michigan Indians telling of the origin of many of Michigan's recognizable landmarks and tourist attractions?

Preparation for All Activities

1. Classroom/school resource: A wall map of Michigan will complement the activities and maps of this lesson.
2. Display a current map of Michigan on the board. Ask a student to come up to the board and show the class where she/he lives in Michigan.
3. Ask the class, "Where do you think Indians live in Michigan?" Have several students place markers, such as sticky notes, on areas where they think Indians live.
4. Lesson the Third provides complementary facts and information, especially Part 3: Negotiating an Indian Treaty and Part 4: Tribes, States, and the U.S. Government: Treaty Rights Lost and Won Back.

PART 1 ▶ LOCATION OF INDIAN LAND IN THE STATE OF MICHIGAN

Introduction

Appended Resources, 4.1 to 4.21, help to show the location of Michigan's Indian people and lands. "Relative Positions of Michigan Indian Villages, circa

1760" (4.1); "Digitally Enhanced Version of the 1837 Schoolcraft Map" (4.2); and "Locator Map of Federally Recognized American Indian Tribes (2000)" (4.3) give a visual representation of the locations of Michigan's Indians during three time periods. An examination of the three maps shows that the relative locations of tribal villages, reservations, and central agencies have remained the same over a 240-year span. Many of Michigan's Native American communities remain relatively near homelands, albeit on lands much reduced in square acreage.

Despite this image of continuity and persistence, the historical maps do not show how and why Native American people moved from place to place or concentrated in particular locales, especially after 1865. Tribes hold lands "reserved" in treaty agreements (today called *reservations*) collectively, while tribal people individually are free to move from place to place. By the 1900s, Michigan's Native Americans converged in such major cities as Grand Rapids, Kalamazoo, Flint, and Detroit; after 1945, the immigration to Michigan of Native Americans from every other state and Canada increased dramatically. They settled mostly in urban areas, but many found employment on Michigan's Indian reservations. History book maps do not show these movements and concentrations, and the juxtaposition between reservation land and population density on maps reveals some interesting contradictions.

First, when a map is designed to show Indian land, governments, and economic activities, location is more important than population. For instance, reservations, bingo halls, and casinos are located in rural or semi-rural areas, leading to the false belief that these areas are where most Indians live (see "American Indian and Other Casinos, circa 2000" [4.5]). This belief is not surprising when the common logic is as follows: If Michigan's Indians have their own land base (the reservations), that must be where they live.

Second, population-density maps such as "Absolute Michigan Indian Population by County, 1990 Census (Numerical)" (4.12), and "Absolute Michigan Indian Population by County, 1990 Census (Choropleth)" (4.15), show that the highest absolute numbers of Indians live in urban areas. But when relative populations are examined (see "Michigan Indian Populaton as a Percentage of County Population, 1990 Census (Numerical)" [4.13], and "Michigan Indian Population as a Percentage of County Population, 1990 Census (Choropleth)" [4.16]) the highest numbers occur in rural areas.

These shifts make for interesting discussion. Most importantly, Michigan's Indians have adapted to changing economic, political, and technological developments while maintaining relationships and interactions within both reservation and urban environments.

- To show the location of Indian land, historical tribal villages, and modern tribal agencies in Michigan.
- To demonstrate that Michigan Indians' reserved lands are relatively close to historical tribal villages and historical centers of trade and subsistence.
- To show why the common understanding of where Michigan Indian casinos are located demonstrates an unknowing understanding of Indian reserved lands and treaty rights.
- To map Michigan Indian population using the Schoolcraft map and the population statistics it reports.
- To map Michigan Indian population using the 1990 U.S. census statistics.
- To identify Michigan Indian population densities in 1837 and compare them to Indian population densities in 1990.
- To identify the Michigan counties with the absolute highest and lowest Indian populations and the highest Indian populations as a percentage of county population.

Activity A ▶ Finding Michigan Indian Villages, circa 1760

Preparation

① Photocopy or create an overhead color transparency for "Relative Positions of Michigan Indian Villages, circa 1760" (4.1).

② Point out the spelling of *Outaouais, Potouatomais, Otchipwe,* and *Nation du Sault* as well as any other words you find interesting.

③ Provide the following information to the class as a whole. The red triangles show the location of Indian villages. Because this is an early French map, the red crosses indicate the location of Jesuit missions and churches, and the fleurs-de-lis locate the relative positions of forts and larger European settlements.

Questions for Thought and Discussion

① Why are the villages located near rivers or the Great Lakes shorelines?

② What is the Seven Years War most often called in U.S. history books?

③ Because (4.1) is based on a map created before the Seven Years War, what language is the map written in?

④ Can you identify or describe the relative locations where the Ottawas, Potawatomis, and Chippewas lived?

⑤ Do the relative locations of Indian populations correspond to your understanding of where they live now?

Activity B ▶ Examining the Schoolcraft Map of 1837

Preparation

① Photocopy or create overhead color transparencies of "Digitally Enhanced Version of the 1837 Schoolcraft Map" (4.2); "Schoolcraft's 1837 Indian Population Estimates" (4.7); and "Michigan Indian Population Statistics from the 1990 U.S. Census by County" (4.11).

② Point out the relative Indian populations, 1837 and 1990. [8,000 and 56,000]

③ Ask when Michigan became a state. [1837]

④ The color-coded areas of (4.2) are lands "reserved" for Michigan's Indians.

⑤ Share the following information with students: Henry Schoolcraft (1789–1865) spent most of his life on Michigan's frontier. He was superintendent of Michigan and served for twenty years as Indian agent to the Chippewas of Sault Ste. Marie and Mackinaw.

⑥ Share the following information with students: Schoolcraft wrote on the map information about who ceded what lands and carefully showed where reserved lands were intended to be located. He also provided population statistics. The treaty provisions were not carried out (e.g., the Grand Traverse Reserve was actually Old Mission Peninsula). For a more detailed biography, have students read Richard G. Bremer's *Indian Agent and Wilderness Scholar: The Life of Henry Rowe Schoolcraft* (1988).

Questions for Thought and Discussion

① Do you think Schoolcraft's "reservations" look too large for the relative population of 8,000 Indians in 1837 and too small for the relative population of 56,000 in 1990?

② For 1837, would you say Michigan Indians lived in relatively rural or isolated areas? How many major cities are shown on the map?

③ In a very basic estimate, what percentage of Michigan land is set aside for Indians? What percentage is set aside for American settlement?

④ Why was Schoolcraft required to make a map of Michigan Indian land cessions, of Indian population, and of the size and location of reserved lands?

Preparation

① Photocopy or create overhead color transparencies for "Federally Recognized American Indian Tribes (2000)" (4.3), and "Comparison of Schoolcraft and Locator Maps" (4.4).

② Ask students if they know of any Indian reservations in their home counties. Then ask them to name the reservations. Not knowing official names is common, but extracting what information students have is useful. Record this information on the board.

③ Share the following information with students: (4.3) names and locates Michigan's American Indian tribal governments and federally recognized reservations in specific ways and places. Point out the use of the noun *Indian* in the official designation of federally recognized tribal entities.

④ Share the following information with students: The U.S. Constitution also uses the noun *Indian*.

⑤ [An interesting bit of information not directly related to this activity is the circle with the four colors used to indicate location. It represents the "circle of life" and the four sacred directions of the Native American people of Michigan.]

Questions for Thought and Discussion

① Consider the official titles and disregard the use of the noun *Indian* for now. What is the relevance of the other terms used—for example, *Bay Mills, Little Traverse Bay,* and *Saginaw?*

② Comment on the significance of the words *community* and *band.* Use a dictionary to get a start.

③ Why is *Indian* used?

④ Notice the use of *Chippewa, Odawa* and *Ottawa,* and *Potawatomi.* Also notice that some "communities" only use the term *Indian.* What do all these designations imply?

⑤ Do Indian reservations exist within counties with major cities, such as Wayne County (Detroit), Genesee County (Flint), or Kent County (Grand Rapids)? Does the location of Indian reservations suggest isolation? Or rural? Perhaps exotic? Explain.

⑥ What comparisons can you make between the 2000 map of "Federally Recognized American Indian Tribes" (4.3) and Schoolcraft's 1837 map (4.2)? Are the locations similar? Compare both to the "Relative Positions" map of 1760 (4.1). Are locations similar? What does the relative position of Indian communities between the maps suggest about consistency over time? How have the names of the Indian communities changed over time?

Activity D ▶ Exploring the Location of Indian Casinos

Preparation

① Photocopy or create overhead color transparencies of "American Indian and Other Casinos, circa 2000" (4.5), and "Comparison of Locator Map to Casino Map" (4.6).

② Ask students if they know about Indian casinos and where they are located. Have one or two students come to the board and identify and/or mark locations on a general map of Michigan.

③ Ask students if they know why Indian communities can build and operate casinos. Then share or review Lesson the Third, Part 4, "Activity C: Casino Gambling."

④ Ask students if they know of any non-Indian-owned and -operated casinos in the state.

⑤ Share the following information with students: Notice the distorted and oversized slot machines used to indicate locations of Indian casinos. The purpose of the distortion is to highlight most non-Indians' image of Indians since Indian communities built their first casinos. Most Indians living in the state do not benefit from casinos, but most people have the opposite impression.

⑥ Share the following information with students: Regardless of the power of symbols and images of casino gambling, people's understanding of where Indian reservations are located has increased as a consequence of the rise of Indian casinos. (Issues of reserved rights and lands and sovereignty can also be explored with the use of an oversized image of a slot machine.)

Questions for Thought and Discussion

① Closely examine "American Indian and Other Casinos, circa 2000" (4.5), and "Comparison of Locator Map to Casinos Map" (4.6). Where are casinos located?

② Do most casinos correspond to the locations of Indian reservations? Why might this relationship exist?

③ The slot machine symbol used to locate Indian casinos is exaggerated for emphasis. What is that emphasis?

④ How can casinos help you to locate Indian reservations? Can casinos help you to understand the concepts of reserved rights and sovereignty? Explain.

Preparation: Graduating Circle Mapping, 1837 Population Estimates

① Photocopy or make an overhead color transparency of "The 1837 Schoolcraft Map for Graduating Circle Mapping" (4.9).

② Photocopy or make overhead color transparencies of the "Instructions for Graduating Circle Mapping" (4.8) and "Schoolcraft's 1837 Indian Population Estimates," (4.7). (4.2) could also be used here as an overhead transparency or photocopied resource to show the origins of Schoolcraft's population statistics.

③ "The Graduating Circle Map of Schoolcraft's 1837 Indian Population Estimates" (4.10), should be saved for postmapping discussion and analysis. Making an overhead transparency of (4.10) is a good way of illustrating results of graduating circle mapping.

④ *Note:* (4.7) is meant to be representational of American Indian population distribution but is not meant to be 100 percent accurate. For greater accuracy, consult Helen Hornbeck Tanner's *Atlas of Great Lakes Indian History* (1987), especially maps 4.23 and 4.25.

⑤ The following steps involve organizing "Schoolcraft's 1837 Indian Population Estimates" (4.7 and 4.10) for each tribal community he identifies:

a. Distribute or show copies of "Schoolcraft's 1837 Indian Population Estimates" (4.7)—one per student or student group. The handout is divided into eight major areas and includes six other Indian communities below the subtotal for a total of fourteen areas for basic graduating circle mapping. Under the subtotal, "Chippewas West of 1836 Land Cession" means west of Marquette and the western Upper Peninsula. For greater accuracy of distribution, the numbers for each of the forty-two communities could be used. (4.10) shows the results and range of this kind of mapping.

b. Have students organize Indian populations in descending order following these groupings: 1,000 and above, 500–600; 300–499; 200–99; 101–99; 100 and below. For basic mapping, they should have fourteen areas to map.

c. Give each student copies of (4.7) and the Schoolcraft map (4.9). Then have students locate the various Indian communities using basic knowledge of Michigan geography.

d. Distribute copies of "Instructions for Graduating Circle Mapping" (4.8). Explain to students how to make graduating circle maps and have students map their data. The handout provides enough "circles" in various colors to map the fourteen population areas (four for 1,000 and above;

two for 500–600; four for 300–99; two for 200–99; one for 101–99; and one for 100 and below). You could also use circle stickers or hand draw circles to the appropriate sizes on the map itself.

Questions for Thought and Discussion: Graduating Circle Mapping

Have students examine the maps they have created then refer to (4.10). After examining the maps, have students answer the following questions.

① What areas of Michigan have the highest concentration of Indian people? Do these areas correspond to the areas of Indian population today? What are the differences?

② In what areas are there no Indians?

③ Where are Indians located? Can you give any geographical information for why Indians might be located in specific places?

④ How evenly or equally is the Indian population distributed around Michigan? In comparison to the choropleth exercise, do you find this distribution today? What are the differences?

⑤ How do reserved lands or reservations (the shaded areas on Schoolcraft's map) correspond to the locations of Indian people? Although the reservations can accommodate the population, can they accommodate the traditional Indian lifestyle (i.e., fishing, hunting, gathering foods such as maple syrup and berries)? Are the reservations too cramped or restrictive? Why or why not?

⑥ Reservations are indicated on the Schoolcraft map. Do reservations exist today in the areas you mapped? Refer to (4.3) to help you decide.

⑦ Look closely at (4.10). What does this map tell you about the locations of Indian populations? Does this map clarify distribution? ([4.16] may help here as well.)

⑧ In comparison to the general graduating circle mapping, in particular the use of various sizes of circles, how is this map better at indicating the locations of Indian populations?

Preparation: Choropleth Mapping, 1990 Census Population Data

① Photocopy or make overhead color transparencies of "Michigan Indian Population Statistics from the 1990 U.S. Census by County" (4.11); "Absolute Michigan Indian Population by County, 1990 Census (Numerical)" (4.12); and "Michigan Indian Population as a Percentage of County Population, 1990 Census (Numerical)" (4.13).

② Photocopy or make an overhead color transparency of "Instructions for Choropleth Mapping" (4.14).

③ Photocopy or make overhead color transparencies of "Absolute Michigan Indian Population by County, 1990 Census (Choropleth)" (4.15), and "Michigan Indian Population as a Percentage of County Population, 1990 Census (Choropleth)" (4.16). Save these resources, along with "Michigan Indian Population Statistics from the 1990 U.S. Census by County" (4.11), for post mapping discussion and analysis. Making overhead color transparencies of (4.15) and (4.16) is a good way of illustrating the results of choropleth mapping.

④ *Note:* (4.15) and (4.16) are meant to be representational of American Indian population distribution according to the 1990 census. Though every effort has been made to use accurate data, the maps are not meant to be 100 percent accurate. Choropleth mapping is meant to show patterns based on a range of information rather than on the actual population of each county. If we mapped by actual figures, we would have to use a different color for each of Michigan's eighty-two counties, which would not show patterns. For absolute accuracy for individual counties, consult the 1990 or 2000 census data.

⑤ The following steps involve organizing the 1990 Michigan Indian Population Statistics:

a. Distribute or show copies of (4.12) and (4.13).

b. Have students identify the counties with the greatest Indian populations. Have students identify the counties with the greatest percentage of Indian population. Discuss the locations identified.

c. Explain to students how to make choropleth maps. Have students map their data using the choropleth guidelines. One map will show absolute Michigan Indian population by county, and a second will show Indian population as a percentage of county population.

Questions for Thought and Discussion: Choropleth Mapping

Have students examine the maps they have created and/or refer to (4.15) and (4.16). After examining the maps, have students answer the following questions.

① Which counties have the highest Indian population? What are the relative locations of those counties?

Some of these include Wayne (8,048), Macomb (2,639), Oakland (3,948), Washtenaw (1,076), Kalamazoo (1,017), Muskegon (1,338), Isabella (1,020), Mackinaw (1,691), Chippewa (3,820), Delta (809), Marquette (943), and Baraga (918) counties, an almost equal split between urban/city population and rural/reservation population.

② Which counties have the highest percentage of Indians? What are the relative locations of those counties?

Isabella (1.9%), Benzie (1.9%), Leelanau (2.7%), Charlevoix (1.8%), Emmet (2.7%), Cheybogan (2.2%), Mackinaw (15.8%), Chippewa (11%), Schoolcraft (6.2%), Delta (2.1%), Gogebic (1.6%) and Baraga (11.5%) counties, with the highest percentages in the Upper Peninsula and in rural/reservation areas.

③ Notice that the counties in questions 1 and 2 are not the necessarily the same. What are the differences?

The highest ratio of Indian population to overall county population is in rural/reservation areas.

④ Why do so many Indians live in urban counties?

Jobs, government relocation in the 1950s and 1960s. Indians live in urban areas all over the United States and Canada for the same reasons, not just in Michigan.

⑤ Why do so many rural counties have a high percentage of Indians?

Reservations are most often found in rural areas.

⑥ Using (4.4), compare the land areas involved in different Michigan Indian treaties with current Indian populations. What connections do you see or not see? What connections did you expect to see but didn't?

The counties with the highest percentages of Indian populations correspond to the reservations created in 1837. However, most of Michigan's Indians live in urban/city areas, far away from these rural/reservation locations.

⑦ Using (4.4), locate present-day reservations. How does the presence of a reservation affect a county's percentage of Indian population?

Counties with reservations always have greater percentages of Indians.

PART 2 ▶ RELATIONSHIPS AND MOVEMENT WITHIN PLACES: MICHIGAN'S INDIANS INTERACTING WITH THE MICHIGAN LANDSCAPE AND ENVIRONMENT AND THE INFLUENCE OF INDIAN PLACE-NAMES

Introduction

(4.17 to 4.21) show forts, trails, waterways, and highways. The maps depict the movement of Native Americans within the Michigan landscape, showing how their movements had purpose and design and demonstrating an interaction and dependence on more than one place and location for subsistence and social/

ceremonial interaction. Where people grow crops; hunt; fish; gather rice, berries, and honey; make sugar from sugar maples; trade for crafts and goods; and hold powwows or participate in ceremonies associated with the changing seasons. As highways replaced Indian trails and ships and boats took advantage of Michigan's waterways, the traditional water and land routes continued to move Native Americans from one place to another but not always for the same reasons.

Michigan's great cities developed at social and economic crossroads within the state. In particular, Detroit, Flint, and Grand Rapids became the centers of Michigan's industrial revolution, with historical Indian highways and waterways aiding the growth of these population centers. Because of these changing social and economic patterns of living, Michigan's Native Americans, like many other citizens of the state, had to supplement traditional forms of subsistence with modern work and activities, becoming loggers, factory workers, mail carriers, teachers, and lawyers, to name just a few occupations. The traditional routes and byways guided them to their new jobs, often in far-off places. By nature, Native Americans have always been commuters. They travel back and forth to well-remembered places and time-honored homecomings, whether in the city or on the reservation. They bring their culture and traditions to the city and the culture and traditions of the city to the reservation, adapting, exchanging, and changing as always.

Native American interactions with environments outside their reservations are not well understood because most non-Indians perceive Indians as static. Indians are frozen on the reservation because the reservation is where most people believe Indians live. Maps help to perpetuate this idea. Worse, Indians are often frozen in time, perceived as historical artifacts or objects of the past, remembered only in place-names that leave an indelible signature of Euro-American occupation because they originated from non-Indian sources and decision making. Henry Schoolcraft started a trend in 1832 by proposing that many of Michigan's counties be given "Indian" names. These are documented in Virgil Vogel's *Indian Place Names in Michigan* (1986). Place-names perpetuate the notion that Indians are a people of the past or are at best a remnant and perhaps insignificant people. "Indian and Pseudo-Indian County Names" (4.26), offers an idea of the frequency of Indian place-names: thirty-three of Michigan's eighty-two counties have Indian or pseudo-Indian names.

Conversely, by identifying place-names and understanding their influence on thinking, we can enjoy the tribute they pay to Native Americans' role and place in Michigan history. First, however, we must analyze, even on a very simple level, and categorize the origin of Indian place-names. The categories can have many interesting allusions and at times can obscure our understanding of who is who. For example, as Vogel puts it, some of Michigan's Indian place-names are "artificial Indian names," like Alcona; some are "names from literature and legend," like Hiawatha township or Hiawatha village in Schoolcraft County; and some are "other personal names," like Osceola (1803–1838), a Seminole "with nothing at all to do with Michigan history." At least Tecumseh, the Shawnee warrior (1768–1813), traveled to Michigan to solicit help from the Ottawa, Chippewa and Potawatomi to prevent any more land cessions to the fledgling United States. The creation of a greater context and understanding of names enables students to appreciate their role and significance in Michigan history, even if these names have only indirect links to Michigan's Indians or are not related at all.

Objectives

- To understand the relationship between historic Indian trails in Michigan and today's current transportation routes.
- To identify ways in which Indians continue to use trails (or highways) to sustain their cultural traditions and subsistence (work).
- To ascertain the relationship between modern highways and Indian trails.
- To understand why water routes are important to both past and present Indians.
- To understand how Indian place-names influence thinking.
- To understand the prominence and significance of Indian place-names in the context of location.

Preparation

1. Photocopy or make overhead color transparencies of "Forts, 1763" (4.17); "Indian Trails, 1763" (4.18); "Major Waterways, 1763" (4.19); "Major Highways, 1990" (4.20); and "Waterways, Highways, and Byways" (4.21).

2. Ask the students, "How many of you have been hiking in the woods?" Allow students to share such experiences. Next, ask the students, "How did you know where to go?" Some student responses will include following trails, paths in the grass, or signs. Share with students that long before cars existed, Indians traveled using the same trails year after year.

3. Have students locate the forts on (4.17). Ask students if these locations correspond to the locations of cities.

4. Have the students locate the Indian trails on (4.18). Explain that these were some of the main trails that the Indians of Michigan used. Ask the students if they notice anything about the trails.

⑤ Have the students locate rivers and waterways on (4.19). Ask students how waterways could be used as transportation routes.

⑥ Direct the students' attention to the location of highways and roads on (4.20). Have students share their observations.

⑦ (4.21) synthesizes the information of (4.17) to (4.20). This map shows relationships.

Activity A ▶ Forts and Cities

Questions for Thought and Discussion

① Why are forts located where they are? How are they accessed?

② What are forts used for? Whom are they meant to protect?

③ Forts are the initial locations of Euro-American settlement. Most historical maps used in public school classrooms do not indicate Indian settlements. Why not?

④ Using (4.1), (4.15), and (4.16) to help, are forts located near Indian settlements? Why or why not?

⑤ What cities are now located where forts used to be? Which city is the most prominent (has the greatest population)? Explain.

Activity B ▶ Indian Trails in Michigan

Questions for Thought and Discussion

① Why do you think Michigan Indians chose to use their routes over and over again?

② Why do you think there are more trails in the Detroit area?

③ Where are trails located in the Upper Peninsula? Why are there fewer trails in the Upper Peninsula?

④ Study (4.1) and (4.2). How do Indian trails correspond to the locations of Indian populations in 1760 and 1837? Are the locations of Indian populations connected by trails?

⑤ List as many observations as you can make about Indian trails in Michigan.

Activity C ▶ Waterways, Highways, and Byways

Questions for Thought and Discussion

① Compare the Indian trails on (4.18) with the locations of rivers and major waterways on (4.19). What observations do you have now?

② Study (4.1) and (4.2). How do major waterways correspond to the locations of Indian populations in 1760 and 1837? Are the locations of Indian populations connected by waterways (rivers and lakes)?

③ In 1760 and 1837, how do Indians travel by water? What is their mode of transportation?

④ Why do you think Indian trails eventually became roads and highways?

⑤ How would the Indians of today use roads and highways? What would be their purpose?

⑥ Study (4.21). How would Indians travel to Michigan's major cities? Why would they make this trip?

⑦ Using (4.21), what are the relationships between Indian trails, water routes, and highways?

Activity D ▶ Indian Place-Names in Michigan

Preparation

① Divide the students into five teams. Give each team a photocopy of map 18, "County Map of Michigan" (4.25). Use a wall map of Michigan if you have one.

② Make an overhead transparency of (4.26) for post activity discussion.

③ Distribute "Henry Schoolcraft Summary and Great Lake States with Indian Names" (4.24). Ask students to study the definitions.

④ Refer students to a current wall map of Michigan. Have them practice finding their hometowns and other cities on the map. Ask them how they think places such as towns and cities got their names. Ask them to name the counties in which their hometowns are located. Do they know how the counties got their names? Tell students that many of the names of places come from other languages, including Indian languages. Share with the students the information on Henry Schoolcraft provided in this lesson. Tell students that Schoolcraft was instrumental in naming Michigan's eighty-two counties.

⑤ Distribute to students the "Indian Place-Names in Michigan" (4.23) with a list of county names. There is no need to do all counties. Have students work in teams or as a class to decide whether they think each name is an Indian name or not. If not an Indian name, have students guess where the name came from. Have students keep track of their responses (make it into a quiz, if you prefer). Using the master sheet provided, share with students the answers to how the different counties got their names. (For older students, assign each student or teams of students to research the origin of one of the names.) Have the students share their findings with the class.

6. Have students refer to a road map of Michigan or to the wall map of Michigan to locate these places on the copies of the county map. Younger students can draw pictures of Indian translations on sticky notes and post them next to the places on the road map.

7. Have students plan a trip that takes them from their hometown through eight of the Indian-named places on the list. Students should then find the mileage of the trip by using a ruler and the mileage scale on the map.

8. Have students write detailed directions for how to get from one county to the next via land, via water, and using modern highways. When all the directions are done, have students read their directions, leaving out place-names, to a classmate, who will try to repeat the trip.

Questions for Thought and Discussion

1. Did it seem easy or difficult to identify Indian-named places? Why do you think it was easy/difficult?

2. If you could rename your town, what would you rename it, and why?

3. Does the name given to a place have a relationship to the location of the place? Give an example.

4. Do any of the Indian names make sense in terms of the location of Indian villages, reservations, or population concentrations?

   Ottawa, Chippewa, and Saginaw Counties are revealing in this respect.

5. How many counties are named after Indian warriors? Are these Indian warriors from Michigan?

   Three of the four were from Michigan: Osceola (1803–1838) was a famous Seminole chief from Florida, Missaukee was an Ottawa signer of the 1833 Treaty of the Maumee, Mecosta was a Potawatomi signer of the 1836 Treaty of Washington, Newaygo was an Ottawa signer of the 1836 Treaty of Washington.

6. How many counties are named for Indian people? Are these people Michigan Indians?

   See question 5.

7. Some of the names are pseudo-Indian names, meaning that they are meant to sound like or represent Indian language but are inventions. Henry Schoolcraft invented most of these names, like Alcona. Did you mark *yes* on the worksheet for a county you later learned was a Schoolcraft invention? If so, why? Is the yes answer correct? Explain. How are these inventions believable?

   Schoolcraft's creations include Alpena, Oscoda, Kalkaska, Tuscola, and Allegan.

8. Can you invent your own "Indian-sounding" name? How easy/difficult is this task?

⑨ Why name places with Indian words or parts of words?

⑩ Was it easy for your classmate to follow your directions? How could you have written them better to make them easier to follow?

PART 3 ▶ HOW MICHIGAN'S LAND CESSION TREATIES AND INDIAN RESERVATIONS CREATE UNIQUE REGIONS WITHIN THE STATE

Introduction

(4.27) to (4.29) and (4.31) are treaty land cession maps. Land cession maps show the conquest and subjugation of Native American tribes through a visual representation of U.S. appropriation and possession of Indian land as explained in this lesson's introduction. "Puzzle Pieces" (4.27), stresses the point by creating puzzle pieces out of a map depicting Michigan's nine major land cession treaties in color-coded fashion. The eighty-two county borders visible in "Major American Indian Land Cessions by Treaty with County Borders" (4.29), further the point by subdividing the Michigan landscape into Western forms of landownership and political and economic organization as prescribed in the Northwest Ordinance of 1787. The ordinance showed how states could be surveyed and created using a patterned order of settlement through a system of relatively equal-sized counties. Hence, the state of Michigan was officially established by putting together carefully surveyed and visually represented "pieces" on a map, pieces representing first large treaty land cessions and second smaller, square counties.

In technical geographic terms, color-coding treaty land cessions and representing county borders create a new sociological, political, and economic region. The color coding shows, within a twenty-nine-year period, the rapid acquisition of Indian land and the subsequent formation of the state in 1837. The creation of the state could then become a significant contribution to the growing United States. Statehood occurred after the 1836 Treaty of Washington, even though the surveying and naming of counties, the acquisition of more Indian land in the western Upper Peninsula, and the settling of border disputes with neighboring states and territories took another twenty years or so. The goal was to extinguish Indian title to land as quickly as possible and thereby expedite its transformation into a legitimate area of American settlement, where a new culture, with its own way of doing things, could emerge to overwhelm the old.

Michigan's Native Americans and their tribal governments negotiated via the treaty process to retain autonomous tracts of land where their cultures, governments, and societies could endure. Because Native Americans were not completely isolated, as part 2 of this lesson confirms, the reservations created pockets of Native American survival and change. Color-coding treaty land cessions and drawing in the four-sided boundaries of eighty-two counties demonstrate the power of visual imagery in historical thinking. In the same way, the symbols and color coding that represent villages, reservations, tribal agencies, and casino operations on maps (4.1) to (4.5) and (4.29) show how and why Michigan Native Americans remain viable cultural entities.

Objectives

- To demonstrate how Indian treaties are state-building instruments.
- To show the east-to-west process of acquiring Indian land.
- To enable students to name the major land cession treaties that led to Michigan statehood: the 1807 Treaty of Detroit; the 1819 Treaty of Saginaw, Michigan Territory; the 1821 Treaty of Chicago, Illinois; and the 1836 Treaty of Washington, D.C. (A complete list of treaties associated with Michigan is appended for reference, historical accuracy, and post-activity discussion. (4.27) to (4.31) depict the nine major land cession treaties.)
- To enable students to understand that negotiating and signing treaties is the first step in creating a state. After Indian land was acquired through the treaty-making process, counties could be surveyed, named, settled, and politically/economically organized.
- To enable students to identify and locate major Michigan Indian treaties in time and place.

Preparation

1. Photocopy "Major American Indian Land Cessions by Treaty, with County Borders" (4.29), and/or make an overhead color transparency of the map. The "Complete List of Michigan Indian Treaties" is provided if you want complete accuracy (4.30). Indicate to students that the nine treaties depicted in (4.27) to (4.31) are the major land cession treaties. After the negotiation and signing of these treaties, especially the 1836 Treaty of Washington, D.C., Michigan had "bought" enough land to become a state.

2. (4.27) to (4.31) can be used in conjunction with Lesson the Third, especially activities 2 and 3. Review the "Supreme Law of the Land" (Article 6, paragraph 2 of the U.S. Constitution) section in Lesson the Third.

3. Using (4.29), go over the nine treaties in chronological order, indicating dates and names. Have students study this information.

④ Have students study the land area acquired by each treaty. Ask students to identify which treaty or treaties acquired the land for their hometowns or counties.

⑤ Tell students that Michigan became a state in 1837 as a direct result of these land acquisitions.

Activity A ▶ How Maps Show Treaties as Land-Acquisition Instruments and State-Building Documents

Preparation

① Photocopy "Puzzle Pieces" (4.27), for each student or student group.

② Carefully cut out the puzzle pieces.

③ Have students glue the pieces onto 8½" by 11" sheets of paper.

④ Have students assemble the state of Michigan in chronological order. If necessary, consult "Puzzle Pieces (Assembled)" (4.28) for help.

⑤ Have students discuss how treaties build states.

Alternatively, photocopy (4.28) and (4.29) for each student or student group and have students examine the treaty pieces in comparison to the complete picture. (4.28) and (4.29) may also be used in a lecture format to achieve the same end.

Questions for Thought and Discussion

① How many years did it take for Michigan to become a state?
Starting with the creation of the Michigan Territory in 1805, followed by the 1807 Treaty of Detroit and ending with the 1836 Treaty of Washington, thirty-one years and seven land-acquisition treaties were required before Michigan could become a state.

② After the March 28, 1836 Treaty of Washington, enough Indian land (the whole Lower Peninsula) had been acquired to create the state of Michigan. How were treaty negotiators able to proceed with statehood without the western portion of the Upper Peninsula?
This rural, out-of-the-way land was not as important as the land of the eastern Upper Peninsula and Lower Peninsula.

③ What is the general direction (or flow) of treaties and land acquisition. East to west? Southeast to northwest? What does this flow of land acquisition reveal about how American history is taught?
East to west. American history is most often taught in an east-to-west fashion: Pilgrims landing on the eastern shore, colonies created, Daniel Boone settling the Ohio Valley, the Overland trail to Oregon, and so forth.

④ Is the general image of American history an east-to-west progression? Why or why not?

Activity B ▶ Native American Land Cessions by Treaty and County Borders:
How Maps Create Borders

Preparation

① Photocopy or make an overhead color transparency of "Major American Indian Land Cessions by Treaty, with County Borders" (4.29). Study the map and review Preparation for Part 3 (All Activities) on page 152.

Questions for Thought and Discussion

① How many major land cession treaties were there? How many years did the treaty-making process take?
Nine; thirty-five years.

② How were the lands legally acquired? What is the first step in the state-building process?
Answer to both questions is treaties.

③ Why are treaties necessary? Why not just take the land? What legal foundation do treaties establish?
The United States requires legal status for land to be bought and sold. (See Lesson the Third for more information.)

④ Name the four treaties that acquired the most land for state-building purposes. What one treaty acquired the most land? When did Michigan become a state? Explain any relationships or connections between treaties and state building.
1807 Treaty of Detroit, 1819 Treaty of Saginaw, 1821 Treaty of Chicago, and 1836 Treaty of Washington, which also acquired the most land.

Activity C ▶ County Borders and the Birth of a State:
A Short Test of Knowledge

Preparation

① Photocopy or make an overhead transparency of "Major County/Treaty Borders" (4.31). Study "Major American Indian Land Cessions by Treaty, with County Borders" (4.29), and review Preparation for Part 3 (All Activities) on page 152.

② Use (4.31) to quiz students on their knowledge of Indian land-acquisition treaties.

Questions for Thought and Discussion

1. Find the county in which you live and name the treaty or treaties that enabled your county to be created.

2. Why are counties an important part, or component, of states? What political, social, or economic purpose do counties serve? Like land cessions and treaties, are counties building blocks of states? How?

   Counties allow for local control of political and social institutions. A greater number of counties allows for greater democracy, as more people have a say in how their local communities are governed. Each of the eighty-two counties is an integral part of the state.

3. Name the four major land cession treaties on (4.31). Name all nine for additional credit. If you'd prefer, color-code the treaties as you identify them.

   1807 Treaty of Detroit, 1819 Treaty of Saginaw, 1821 Treaty of Chicago, and 1836 Treaty of Washington. The others are the 1817 Treaty of the Maumee, 1828 Treaty of St, Joseph River, 1833 Treaty of Chicago, 1836 Treaty of Cedar Point, and 1842 Treaty of LaPointe.

PART 4 ▶ DIFFERENT WAYS OF MAPPING CULTURE AND HISTORY

Introduction

"Ojibwa Migration Chart" (4.34), "An Example of 'Word Pictures' Depicting American Popular Culture" (4.35), and "Mapping a Story with Pictographs" (4.36) are not ordinary maps. They demonstrate an alternative way of mapping. Mapping is not always about precise location, directions, or American history; maps are sometimes constructed of pictures or symbols that are meant as representations of individual invention, visual memory, and/or stories linked to geographic settings. Michigan Indians use pictures etched and drawn on wood, rock, parchment, paper, and canvas to record cultural traits, family history, songs, visions, and stories. Some of oldest forms of this style of mapping can be found in what archaeologists call pictographs, which are recognizable images etched in stone. Pictographs are still used today. Even the maps you recognize as maps use pictures to symbolize highways, forts, rivers, and lakes, among other features. Maps often include legends to identify and explain the pictures used to represent details and specifics. In other cases, people must rely on cultural knowledge to decipher the pictures, symbols, and images on maps. "An Example of 'Word Pictures' Depicting American Popular Culture" (4.35), should make the meaning of *cultural knowledge* clear.

The "Ojibwa Migration Chart" (4.34) (on exhibit at the Museum of Ojibwe Culture, St. Ignace, Michigan) and accompanying information allow non-Indian people to begin an interpretation of one version of the Ojibwe origin and migration story without the need for a lot of cultural knowledge about Michigan Chippewa history and people. Michigan Chippewas who know their oral and pictorial tradition do not need words to interpret the map, but many Chippewas living today can benefit from a visual and written record of the origins of their people. The rest of us need clues (for example, the words, *Ojibwa Migration Chart*) and pointers to identify places such as Mackinaw and Sault Ste. Marie, Michigan, and Sandy Lake, Minnesota. We also are helped by the glossary of symbols explaining how to detect "bear," "otter," and the "huge fish monster." At the most basic level, the "Ojibwa Migration Chart" is an Indian way of mapping the movement and location of Michigan Indians within the state and beyond. This chart simply does so in a Chippewa manner—an unconventional way of map making. The "Ojibwa Migration Chart" can be viewed as a map that emphasizes lakes and rivers and travel by water. Students can explore the map to expand their knowledge of Chippewa culture but also to explore new ways of imagining the world through alternative ways of mapmaking.

Most of us, from time to time, will create "maps" using pictures or images to identify a feeling or emotion rather than to locate a place. How do you map a special place situated in a specific geographical location to express the feeling rather than the place? How can pictures and images reveal cultural knowledge? This kind of mapping shows how humans are geographic agents and demonstrates a humanistic geography by the creative mapping of culture onto places and locations. The following activities allow students to investigate the possibilities.

Objectives

- To show alternative ways of mapping history and culture.
- To show how symbols and maps can reflect cultural knowledge.
- To show how maps can be stories.
- To demonstrate how maps can be personal or specific to a family or group of people.
- To demonstrate how pictographs or story maps aid our memories of important events and how these events are grounded in location and environment.

Preparation

① Have students read "The Ojibwa Migration Story" (4.32) and the "Glossary of Ojibwa Symbols" (4.33).

② Photocopy or make an overhead color transparency of "Ojibwa Migration Chart" (4.34).

③ Have students study the chart to find images and symbols with which they are familiar by virtue of reading the story and glossary. List the images and symbols they cannot identify. Tell them that the Ojibwa symbols are metaphorical and mnemonic and that Ojibwa elders who have years of cultural knowledge have a greater capacity to interpret these symbols and this journey.

④ *Note:* The goal of the activity is not to understand completely the Ojibwa Migration, origin story, or *MidèWiwin* (Grand Medicine Society) belief system but to understand how these stories and teachings can be symbolized on maps.

Questions for Thought and Discussion

① "Ojibwa Migration Chart" (4.34) flows east to west. How are water or waterways depicted? Why are rivers and lakes important to the migration? The depiction of waterways resembles a road drawn with two parallel lines. When these parallel lines form a circle or oblong shape, a lake forms. Rivers and lakes are the highways of a people traveling by canoe or boat.

② Can you find the "wrong rivers," "Crane," "Bear," and "Otter"? The wrong rivers are the two wavy lines under the A and the M. When you look hard, the shapes of animals are easy to find, especially the turtle.

③ Compare "The Ojibwa Migration Story" to the chart itself. Are they the same? Is there more information on the chart or in the words? How can there be more information on the chart?

④ How would you create your own maps of journeys and travels, imagined or real? What would be most important to you, and how would you symbolize that importance?

⑤ How can maps such as the migration chart help a people remember important events or knowledge? Have students look up the word *mnemonic* to help to answer this question.

⑥ How does the chart depict a moral environment? How does the Pack of Life create a human geography? Good conduct leads to a better life and world.

Preparation

① Photocopy or make an overhead transparency of "An Example of 'Word Pictures' Depicting American Popular Culture" (4.35), to share with students.

② Share the following: *Cultural knowledge* is simply being able to recognize symbols and images and tell a story about them.

③ Have students study "Student Example: The Great and Powerful Shoemaker" for images and symbols they can identify and tell a story about.

④ Have students write or discuss what they know about the various shoes they see on the map.

Questions for Thought and Discussion

① How is "An Example of 'Word Pictures' Depicting American Popular Culture" (4.35) a map? What information does it convey?
Like "The Ojibwa Migration Chart," "Student Example: The Great and Powerful Shoemaker" reveals cultural information that most Americans can recognize. For instance, very few Americans will not recognize ballet slippers, the rabbit slippers, or the wicked witch's shoes sticking out from underneath Dorothy's wind-relocated house. It is a map of what a young girl might learn or know about when asked to draw a picture of her experiences.

② How do the shoes tell a story about our culture or our society?
See question 1.

Preparation

① Photocopy or make an overhead color transparency of "Mapping a Story with Pictographs" (4.36), to share with students.

② Have students create a map showing an adventure, a special vacation, or a journey to some far-off place. Encourage students to not use words of any kind but do not negatively draw attention to students who do. As you can tell, the student example uses "moving van" and "for sale," but the visual story is nevertheless transmitted. Have students create symbols and images others can recognize using colored pencils, crayons, or markers as available.

③ On the back of the paper, have students create a glossary, identifying and defining at least four of the images or symbols used in their depiction.

④ When all students have completed the task, have them present their "stories" to the class or to other students without explaining what they were trying to depict. Allow students to interpret each story based on what they see.

⑤ When presentations are completed, have students use words to explain what they were trying to accomplish.

⑥ Have students make comparisons between the various interpretations and individual student intent. Use "An Example of Student Mapping" (4.37), for comparison.

Questions for Thought and Discussion

① How was your story interpreted? Were others able to "read" your story?

② Did you use images or symbols others could recognize? Could you have used more recognizable symbols? If so, what kind and how would they fit into your story?

③ When you added words (when you explained your depiction), did others have a greater understanding of your intent?

④ How does your pictograph help you to remember an important event or time in your life?

⑤ What is most important about your story, and how is it emphasized in your map?

Activity D ▶ Creating a Map of a Meaningful Place

Preparation

① Have students list at least one very special place (a specific geographical location) that has meaning to them.

② Have students write a paragraph explaining why this place is important and why it has significant meaning.

③ Using colored pencils, crayons, markers, or pens, have students create a map of this place that emphasizes, through images or symbols, the historical or personal importance of this place.

④ The map can be conventional or creative in personal invention. The goal, however, is for others to derive some meaning from the images rendered.

⑤ Discuss the end results of every student map and continue to make comparisons between interpretation and intent.

⑥ Refer to "The Ojibwa Migration Chart" (4.34) to make further comparisons and to generate discussion of alternative ways of mapping.

Questions for Thought and Discussion

❶ How are the maps produced in these activities related to the conventional maps? How do these maps differ?

❷ What have you learned about historical maps?

❸ What is the importance of personal maps, such as the ones created in this lesson, or maps specific to Indian culture?

APPENDED RESOURCES

Part 1: Location of Indian Land in the State of Michigan

(4.1) Relative Positions of Michigan Indian Villages, circa 1760 162

(4.2) Digitally Enhanced Version of the 1837 Schoolcraft Map 163

(4.3) Locator Map of Federally Recognized American Indian Tribes (2000) . 164

(4.4) Comparison of Schoolcraft and Locator Maps 165

(4.5) American Indian and Other Casinos, circa 2000 166

(4.6) Comparison of Locator Map to Casino Map 167

(4.7) Schoolcraft's 1837 Indian Population Estimates 168

(4.8) Instructions for Graduating Circle Mapping 169

(4.9) The 1837 Schoolcraft Map for Graduating Circle Mapping 170

(4.10) The Graduating Circle Map of Schoolcraft's 1837 Indian
Population Estimates 171

(4.11) Michigan Indian Population Statistics from the 1990 U.S. Census
by County 172

(4.12) Absolute Michigan Indian Population by County, 1990 Census
(Numerical) 173

(4.13) Michigan Indian Population as a Percentage of County Population,
1990 Census (Numerical) 174

(4.14) Instructions for Choropleth Mapping 175

(4.15) Absolute Michigan Indian Population by County, 1990 Census
(Choropleth) 176

(4.16) Michigan Indian Population as a Percentage of County Population,
1990 Census (Choropleth) 177

*Part 2: Relationships and Movement within Places: Michigan's Indians
Interacting with the Michigan Landscape and Environment and the
Influence of Indian Place-Names*

(4.17) Forts, 1763 178

(4.18) Indian Trails, 1763 179

(4.19) Major Waterways, 1763 180

(4.20) Major Highways, 1990 181

(4.21) Waterways, Highways, and Byways 182

(4.22) Indian Place-Names in Michigan: Teacher's Master 183

(4.23) Indian Place-Names in Michigan: Worksheet 189

(4.24) Henry Schoolcraft Summary and Great Lake States
     with Indian Names 190

(4.25) County Map of Michigan 191

(4.26) Indian and Pseudo-Indian County Names 192

Part 3: How Michigan's Land Cession Treaties and Indian Reservations
Create Unique Regions within the State

(4.27) Puzzle Pieces 193

(4.28) Puzzle Pieces (Assembled) 194

(4.29) Major American Indian Land Cessions by Treaty
     with County Borders 195

(4.30) Complete List of Michigan Indian Treaties 196

(4.31) Major County/Treaty Borders 197

Part 4: Different Ways of Mapping Culture and History

(4.32) The Ojibwa Migration Story 198

(4.33) Glossary of Ojibwa Symbols 200

(4.34) Ojibwa Migration Chart 201

(4.35) An Example of "Word Pictures" Depicting American Popular
     Culture 202

(4.36) Mapping a Story with Pictographs 203

(4.37) An Example of Student Mapping 204

(4.38) Questions for Thought and Discussion 205

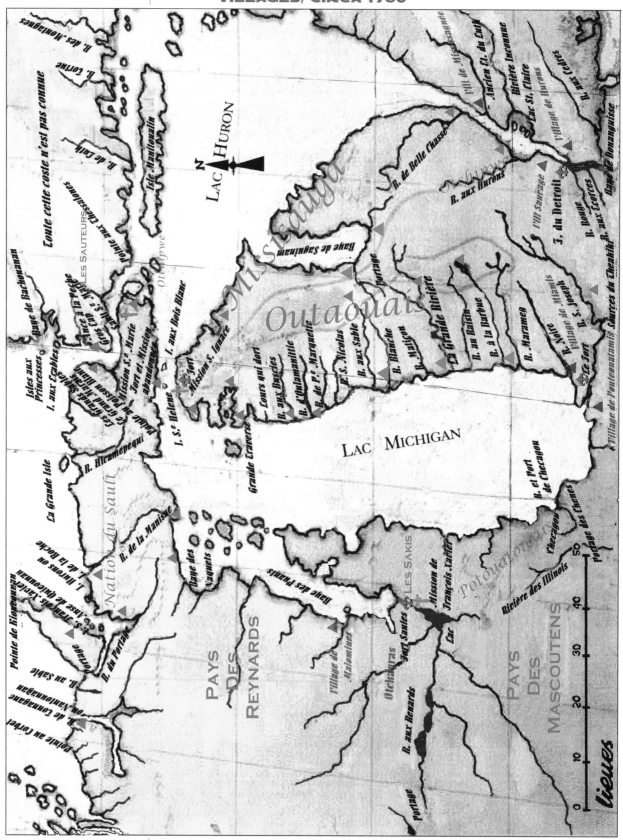

  © PATRICK RUSSELL LEBEAU 2005 / ALL RIGHTS RESERVED

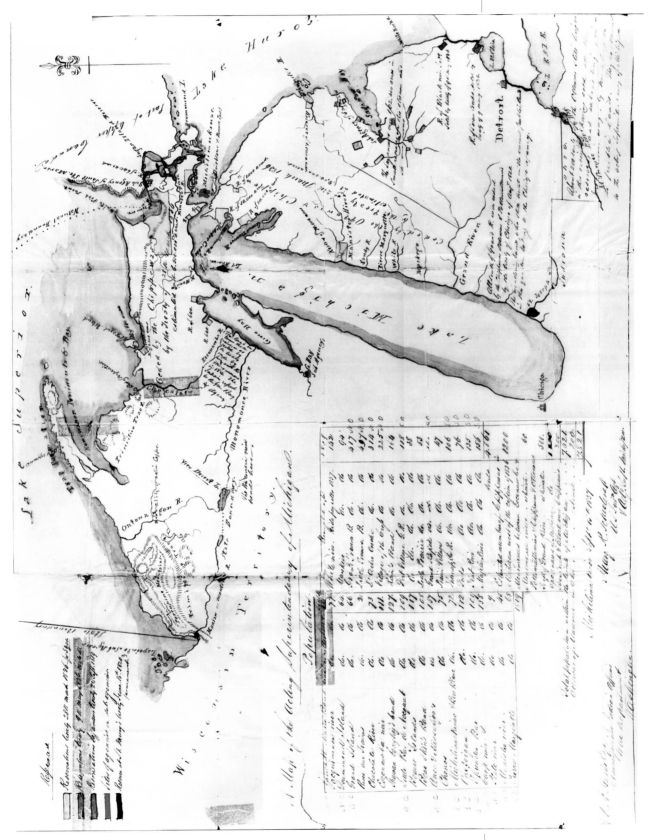

© PATRICK RUSSELL LEBEAU 2005 / ALL RIGHTS RESERVED

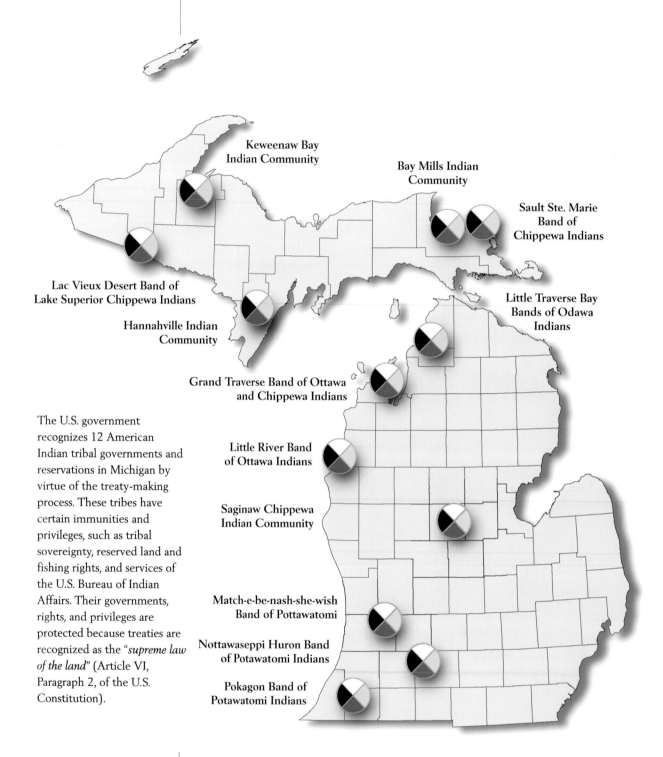

Keweenaw Bay
Indian Community

Bay Mills Indian
Community

Sault Ste. Marie
Band of
Chippewa Indians

Lac Vieux Desert Band of
Lake Superior Chippewa Indians

Little Traverse Bay
Bands of Odawa
Indians

Hannahville Indian
Community

Grand Traverse Band of Ottawa
and Chippewa Indians

Little River Band
of Ottawa Indians

Saginaw Chippewa
Indian Community

Match-e-be-nash-she-wish
Band of Pottawatomi

Nottawaseppi Huron Band
of Potawatomi Indians

Pokagon Band of
Potawatomi Indians

The U.S. government
recognizes 12 American
Indian tribal governments and
reservations in Michigan by
virtue of the treaty-making
process. These tribes have
certain immunities and
privileges, such as tribal
sovereignty, reserved land and
fishing rights, and services of
the U.S. Bureau of Indian
Affairs. Their governments,
rights, and privileges are
protected because treaties are
recognized as the "*supreme law
of the land*" (Article VI,
Paragraph 2, of the U.S.
Constitution).

© PATRICK RUSSELL LEBEAU 2005 / ALL RIGHTS RESERVED

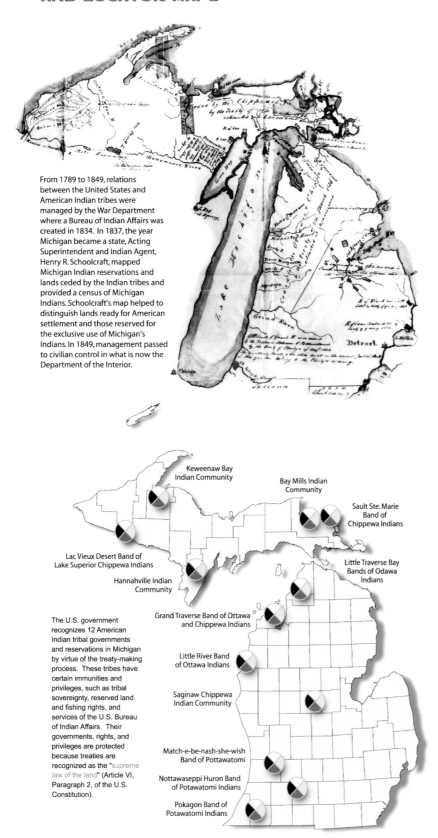

From 1789 to 1849, relations between the United States and American Indian tribes were managed by the War Department where a Bureau of Indian Affairs was created in 1834. In 1837, the year Michigan became a state, Acting Superintendent and Indian Agent, Henry R. Schoolcraft, mapped Michigan Indian reservations and lands ceded by the Indian tribes and provided a census of Michigan Indians. Schoolcraft's map helped to distinguish lands ready for American settlement and those reserved for the exclusive use of Michigan's Indians. In 1849, management passed to civilian control in what is now the Department of the Interior.

Keweenaw Bay
Indian Community

Bay Mills Indian
Community

Sault Ste. Marie
Band of
Chippewa Indians

Lac Vieux Desert Band of
Lake Superior Chippewa Indians

Little Traverse Bay
Bands of Odawa
Indians

Hannahville Indian
Community

The U.S. government recognizes 12 American Indian tribal governments and reservations in Michigan by virtue of the treaty-making process. These tribes have certain immunities and privileges, such as tribal sovereignty, reserved land and fishing rights, and services of the U.S. Bureau of Indian Affairs. Their governments, rights, and privileges are protected because treaties are recognized as the "supreme law of the land" (Article VI, Paragraph 2, of the U.S. Constitution).

Grand Traverse Band of Ottawa
and Chippewa Indians

Little River Band
of Ottawa Indians

Saginaw Chippewa
Indian Community

Match-e-be-nash-she-wish
Band of Pottawatomi

Nottawaseppi Huron Band
of Potawatomi Indians

Pokagon Band of
Potawatomi Indians

© PATRICK RUSSELL LEBEAU 2005 / ALL RIGHTS RESERVED

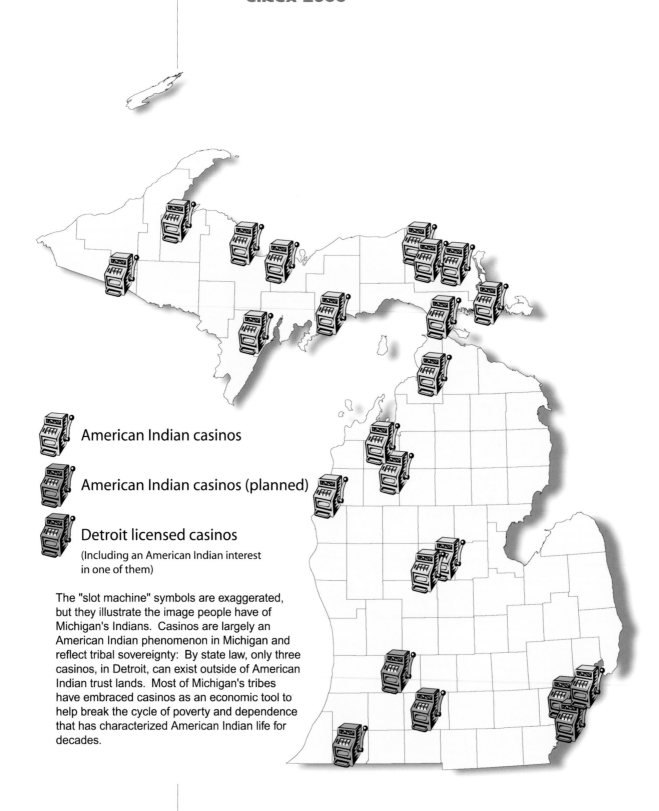

American Indian casinos

American Indian casinos (planned)

Detroit licensed casinos
(Including an American Indian interest
in one of them)

The "slot machine" symbols are exaggerated,
but they illustrate the image people have of
Michigan's Indians. Casinos are largely an
American Indian phenomenon in Michigan and
reflect tribal sovereignty: By state law, only three
casinos, in Detroit, can exist outside of American
Indian trust lands. Most of Michigan's tribes
have embraced casinos as an economic tool to
help break the cycle of poverty and dependence
that has characterized American Indian life for
decades.

 © PATRICK RUSSELL LEBEAU 2005 / ALL RIGHTS RESERVED

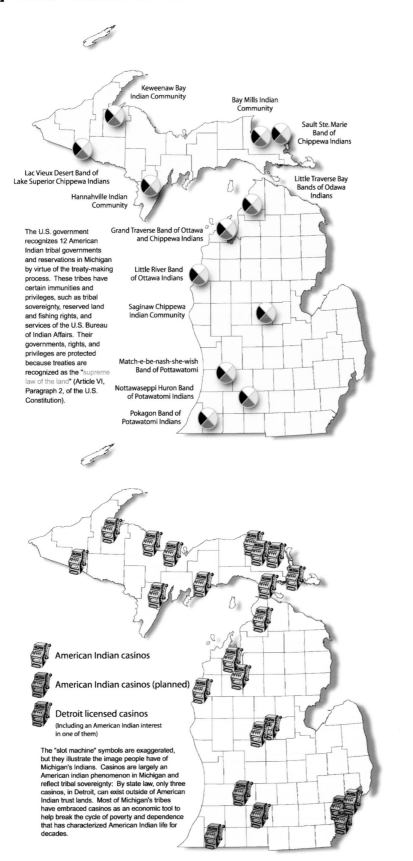

Keweenaw Bay
Indian Community

Bay Mills Indian
Community

Sault Ste. Marie
Band of
Chippewa Indians

Lac Vieux Desert Band of
Lake Superior Chippewa Indians

Little Traverse Bay
Bands of Odawa
Indians

Hannahville Indian
Community

The U.S. government recognizes 12 American Indian tribal governments and reservations in Michigan by virtue of the treaty-making process. These tribes have certain immunities and privileges, such as tribal sovereignty, reserved land and fishing rights, and services of the U.S. Bureau of Indian Affairs. Their governments, rights, and privileges are protected because treaties are recognized as the "supreme law of the land" (Article VI, Paragraph 2, of the U.S. Constitution).

Grand Traverse Band of Ottawa
and Chippewa Indians

Little River Band
of Ottawa Indians

Saginaw Chippewa
Indian Community

Match-e-be-nash-she-wish
Band of Pottawatomi

Nottawaseppi Huron Band
of Potawatomi Indians

Pokagon Band of
Potawatomi Indians

American Indian casinos

American Indian casinos (planned)

Detroit licensed casinos
(Including an American Indian interest
in one of them)

The "slot machine" symbols are exaggerated, but they illustrate the image people have of Michigan's Indians. Casinos are largely an American indian phenomenon in Michigan and reflect tribal sovereignty: By state law, only three casinos, in Detroit, can exist outside of American Indian trust lands. Most of Michigan's tribes have embraced casinos as an economic tool to help break the cycle of poverty and dependence that has characterized American Indian life for decades.

© PATRICK RUSSELL LEBEAU 2005 / ALL RIGHTS RESERVED

Sault Ste. Marie to Drummond Island

Sault Ste Marie Band 180

Tacquimenon River 77

Drummond Island 64

Total 321

Marquette to Grand Island

Grand Island 66

River aux Traines 2

Chocolate River 73

Total 141

Escanaba and Bay de Noc Area

Esconawba noir 111

Shawan Egeeghig's Band? 127

Little Bay de Nocquet 109

Total 347

Straits of Mackinaw Area

Bear Skin's Band? 108

Ance Velliseusigo's 157

Chenos 75

Michilimackinac Bois Blanc 72

Cheboigan 112

Total 524

Alpena Area

Thunder Bay 109

Canfe Noir? 138

Total 247

Along the West Coast of Michigan North of Grand River

Platte River 9

Manistee 45

Pierre Marquette 68

White River 142

Maskigo 94

Total 358

Traverse Bay Area

Grand Traverse Bay 417

Little Traverse Bay 497

L'Arbe Croche 314

Village of the Cross 225

Beaver Islands 117

Total 1,570

Along the Grand River

Rain's Band? 164

Fort Village G.R. 156

Little Prairie G.R. 53

Grand Rapids . . . . 166?

Prairie Village G.R. 47

Thornapple River G.R. 106

Forks G.R. 76

Flat River G.R. 135

Maple River G.R. 150

Total 1,053

Subtotal 4, 561

Chippewas West of 1836
    Land Cession 1,200

Monomonees Between Escanaba
    and Mon. Rivers 60

Three Rivers People South
    of the Grand River 500

Saginaw of Michigan 1,000

Swan Creek and Black River
    Chippewas 300

Total within limits of Michigan . . 7,621

Ottowas of Manumee in Ohio . . 200

Schoolcraft's Grand Total 7,821

© PATRICK RUSSELL LEBEAU 2005 / ALL RIGHTS RESERVED

[4.8] INSTRUCTIONS FOR GRADUATING CIRCLE MAPPING

Graduating Circle Mapping is an easy way of indicating population density in general areas on a map. By using various sized, and color-coded, circles, a map of relative population density can be formed. The circles, however, do not show the distribution of Indian villages over a wider area; the circles are only meant to give students a basic image of Indian population in 1837. To achieve greater accuracy a greater number of smaller circles must be used. Study Schoolcraft's population estimates and determine locations by the 8 groupings and the 6 estimates below the subtotal of student handout of "Schoolcraft's 1837 Indian Population Estimates."

Population Range   **Relative Size of Circle**

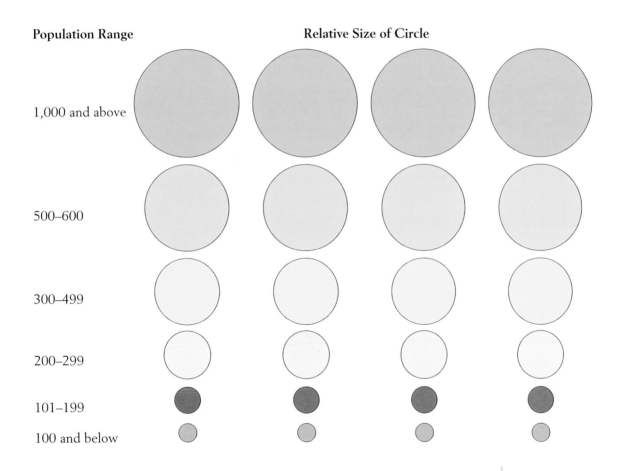

1,000 and above

500–600

300–499

200–299

101–199

100 and below

© PATRICK RUSSELL LEBEAU 2005 / ALL RIGHTS RESERVED

INSTRUCTIONS: Cut out circles found on the "Instructions for Graduating Circle Mapping." Place the appropriate-sized circle in the designated area using "Schoolcraft's 1837 Indian Population Estimates."

© PATRICK RUSSELL LEBEAU 2005 / ALL RIGHTS RESERVED

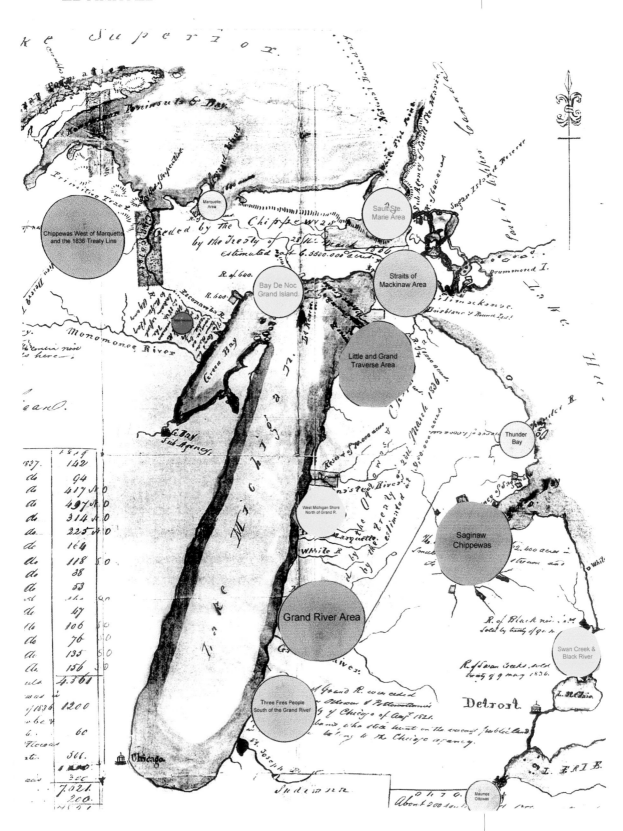

© PATRICK RUSSELL LEBEAU 2005 / ALL RIGHTS RESERVED

[4.11] MICHIGAN INDIAN POPULATION STATISTICS FROM THE 1990 U.S. CENSUS BY COUNTY

County	Total Pop.	Indian Pop.	% Indian Pop.	County	Total Pop.	Indian Pop.	% Indian Pop.
Alcona	10,145	56	0.6	Lake	8,583	81	0.9
Alger	8,972	302	3.4	Lapeer	74,768	318	0.4
Allegan	90,509	541	0.6	Lelanau	16,527	450	2.7
Alpena	30,605	93	0.3	Lenawee	91,476	295	0.3
Antrim	18,185	210	1.2	Livingston	115,645	701	0.6
Arenac	14,931	138	0.9	Luce	5,763	330	5.7
Baraga	7,954	918	11.5	Mackinac	10,674	1,689	15.8
Barry	50,057	188	0.4	Macomb	717,400	2,600	0.4
Bay	111,723	717	0.6	Manistee	21,265	189	0.9
Benzie	12,200	237	1.9	Marquette	70,887	939	1.3
Berrien	1,61,378	676	0.4	Mason	25,537	187	0.7
Branch	41,502	219	0.5	Menominee	24,920	382	1.5
Calhoun	135,982	687	0.5	Menominee	24,920	382	1.5
Cass	49,477	468	0.9	Midland	7,651	333	0.4
Charlevoix	21,468	377	1.8	Missaukee	12,147	74	0.6
Cheboygan	21,398	476	2.2	Monroe	133,600	476	0.4
Chippewa	34,604	3,818	11	Montcalm	53,059	364	0.7
Clare	24,952	156	0.6	Montmorency	8,936	48	0.5
Clinton	57,883	274	0.5	Muskegon	158,983	1,331	0.8
Crawford	12,260	145	1.2	Newaygo	38,202	244	0.6
Delta	37,780	806	2.1	Oakland	1,083,592	3,888	0.4
Dickinson	26,831	130	0.5	Oceana	22,454	233	1
Eaton	92,879	435	0.5	Ogemaw	18,681	140	0.7
Emmet	25,040	676	2.7	Ontonagon	8,854	108	1.2
Genesee	430,459	3,109	0.7	Osceola	20,146	117	0.6
Gladwin	21,896	114	0.5	Oscoda	7,842	41	0.5
Gogebic	18,052	283	1.6	Otsego	17,957	102	0.6
Grand Traverse	64,273	548	0.9	Ottawa	187,768	629	0.3
Gratiot	38,982	143	0.4	Presque Isle	13,743	43	0.6
Hillsdale	43,431	138	0.3	Roscommon	19,776	100	0.3
Houghton	35,446	148	0.4	Saginaw	211,946	898	0.3
Huron	34,951	88	0.3	Sanilac	39,928	194	0.5
Ingham	281,912	1,913	0.7	Schoolcraft	8,302	517	6.2
Ionia	57,042	220	0.4	Shiawassee	69,770	394	0.6
Iosco	30,209	221	0.7	St. Clair	145,607	743	0.5
Iron	13,175	102	0.8	St. Joseph	58,913	221	0.4
Isabella	54,624	1,011	1.9	Tuscola	55,498	336	0.6
Jackson	149,756	646	0.4	Van Buren	70,060	644	0.9
Kalamazoo	233,411	1,007	0.5	Washtenaw	282,937	7,954	0.4
Kalkaska	13,947	111	0.8	Wayne	211,687	7,954	0.4
Kent	500,631	2,744	0.5	Wexford	26,360	176	0.7
Keweenaw	1,701	4	0.2				

© PATRICK RUSSELL LEBEAU 2005 / ALL RIGHTS RESERVED

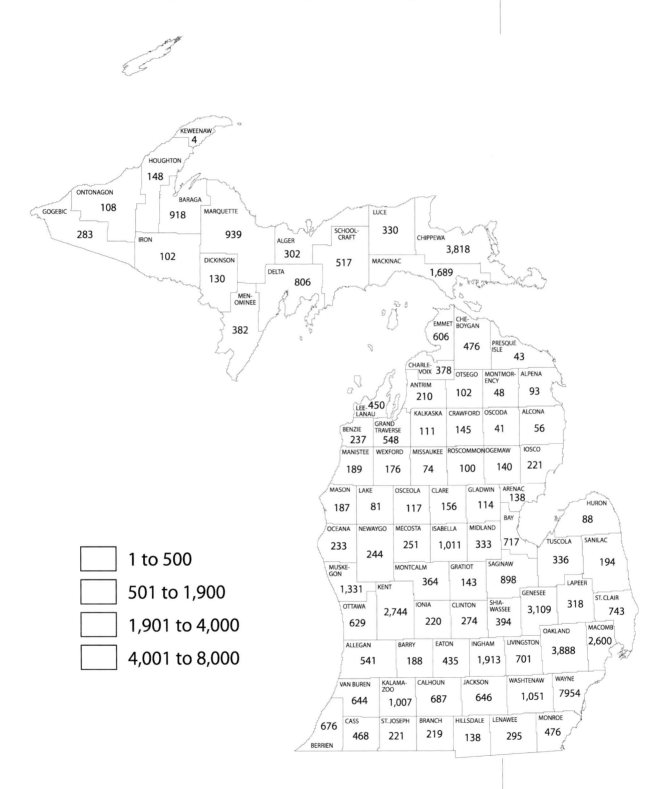

1 to 500

501 to 1,900

1,901 to 4,000

4,001 to 8,000

KEWEENAW
4

HOUGHTON
148

ONTONAGON
108

GOGEBIC
283

BARAGA
918

MARQUETTE
939

IRON
102

DICKINSON
130

ALGER
302

SCHOOL-CRAFT
517

DELTA
806

LUCE
330

CHIPPEWA
3,818

MACKINAC
1,689

MEN-OMINEE
382

EMMET
606

CHE-BOYGAN
476

PRESQUE ISLE
43

CHARLE-VOIX 378

OTSEGO
102

MONTMOR-ENCY
48

ALPENA
93

ANTRIM
210

LEE-LANAU 450

KALKASKA
111

CRAWFORD
145

OSCODA
41

ALCONA
56

BENZIE
237

GRAND TRAVERSE
548

MANISTEE
189

WEXFORD
176

MISSAUKEE
74

ROSCOMMON
100

OGEMAW
140

IOSCO
221

MASON
187

LAKE
81

OSCEOLA
117

CLARE
156

GLADWIN
114

ARENAC
138

HURON
88

OCEANA
233

NEWAYGO
244

MECOSTA
251

ISABELLA
1,011

MIDLAND
333

BAY
717

TUSCOLA
336

SANILAC
194

MUSKE-GON
1,331

KENT
2,744

MONTCALM
364

GRATIOT
143

SAGINAW
898

LAPEER
318

ST. CLAIR
743

OTTAWA
629

IONIA
220

CLINTON
274

SHIA-WASSEE
394

GENESEE
3,109

OAKLAND
3,888

MACOMB
2,600

ALLEGAN
541

BARRY
188

EATON
435

INGHAM
1,913

LIVINGSTON
701

VAN BUREN
644

KALAMA-ZOO
1,007

CALHOUN
687

JACKSON
646

WASHTENAW
1,051

WAYNE
7954

CASS
468

ST. JOSEPH
221

BRANCH
219

HILLSDALE
138

LENAWEE
295

MONROE
476

BERRIEN
676

© PATRICK RUSSELL LEBEAU 2005 / ALL RIGHTS RESERVED

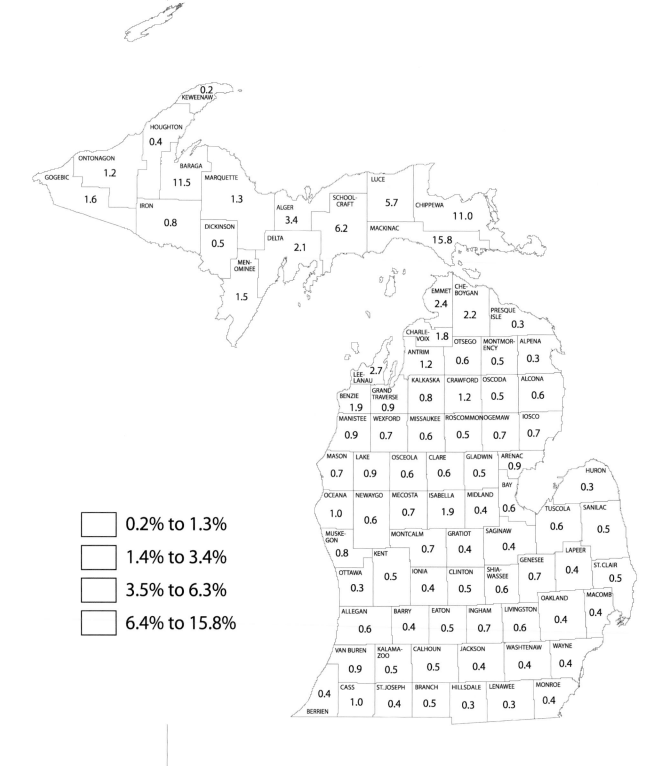

0.2% to 1.3%

1.4% to 3.4%

3.5% to 6.3%

6.4% to 15.8%

© PATRICK RUSSELL LEBEAU 2005 / ALL RIGHTS RESERVED

[4.14] INSTRUCTIONS FOR CHOROPLETH MAPPING

A choropleth map is a map which shows the relative frequency of a certain happening or thing in a specific area. By using varying degrees of darkness of a single color, you can show how often something occurs. For example, red can be shown as light pink, red, and dark red. When using this color, the light pink would show the least number of times something occurs and dark red would show the most number of times. Generally, four groupings are used for choropleth mapping. When you have finished a choropleth map, the map itself would only have varying shades of one color on it.

The mathematical formula for choropleth mapping for this lesson is:

For Total (or absolute) Indian Population by county, use the following breakdown:

Pink	1–500 people
Medium Red	501–1,900 people
Dark Red	1,901–4,000 people
Deep Red	4,001–8,000 people

For Michigan Counties Percentage of Indian Population, use the following breakdown:

Pink	0.2%–1.35%
Medium Red	1.45%–3.4%
Dark Red	3.5%–6.3%
Deep Red	6.4%–15.8%

(Note: Use any color you wish. The shades of red are used for [4.15] and [4.16].)

Total U.S. Indian Population Statistics, 1990 Census

Indian Population, 1890–1990

Date	Size	Change from Prior Decade	Ten States with the Largest American Indian, Eskimo, or Aleut Population, 1990 (In thousands; 1980 rank in parentheses)	Ten States with the Highest Percentage American Indian, Eskimo, or Aleut (1980 rank in parentheses)
1890	248,000			
1990	237,196	–4.5%	Oklahoma (2) 252	Alaska (1) 15.6
1910	276,927	16.8%	California (1) 242	New Mexico (2) 8.9
1920	244,437	–11.7%	Arizona (3) 204	Oklahoma (5) 8.0
1930	343,352	40.5%	New Mexico (4) . . .134	South Dakota (3) . . .7.3
1940	345,252	0.6%	Alaska (6) 86	Montana (6) 6.0
1950	357,4999	3.5%	Washington (7) 81	Arizona(4) 5.6
1960	523,591	46.5%	North Carolina (5) . .80	North Dakota (7) . . .4.1
1970	792,730	51.4%	Texas (9) 66	Wyoming (9) 2.1
1980	1,366,676	72.4%	New York (11) 63	Washington (10) 1.7
1990	1,959,234	37.9%	Michigan (10) 56	Nevada (8) 1.6

© PATRICK RUSSELL LEBEAU 2005 / ALL RIGHTS RESERVED

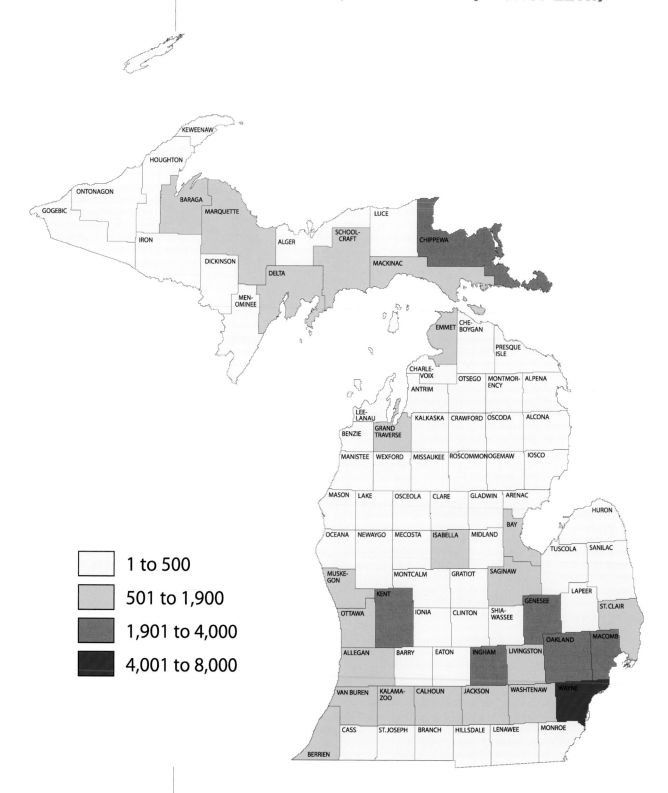

1 to 500

501 to 1,900

1,901 to 4,000

4,001 to 8,000

© PATRICK RUSSELL LEBEAU 2005 / ALL RIGHTS RESERVED

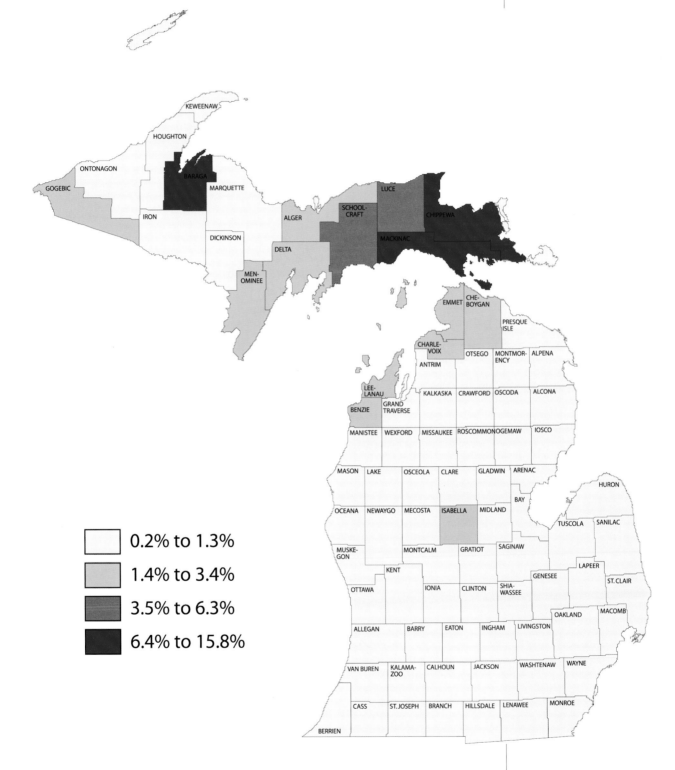

[4.16] MICHIGAN INDIAN POPULATION AS A
PERCENTAGE OF COUNTY POPULATION,
1990 CENSUS (CHOROPLETH)

0.2% to 1.3%

1.4% to 3.4%

3.5% to 6.3%

6.4% to 15.8%

© PATRICK RUSSELL LEBEAU 2005 / ALL RIGHTS RESERVED

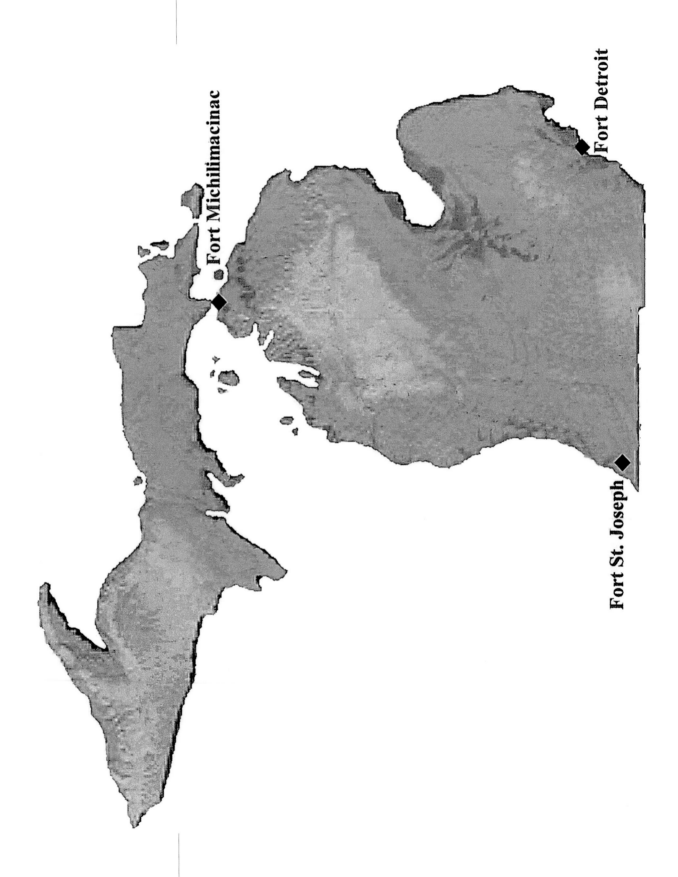

 © PATRICK RUSSELL LEBEAU 2005 / ALL RIGHTS RESERVED

Fort Detroit

Fort Michilimacinac

Fort St. Joseph

Indian Trails

© PATRICK RUSSELL LEBEAU 2005 / ALL RIGHTS RESERVED

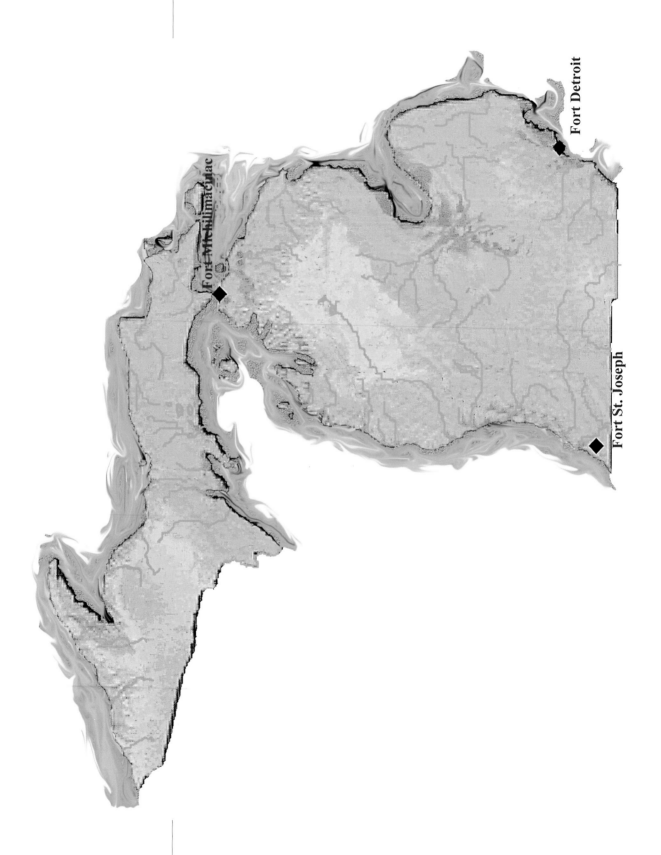

Fort Detroit

Fort Michilimackinac

Fort St. Joseph

© PATRICK RUSSELL LEBEAU 2005 / ALL RIGHTS RESERVED

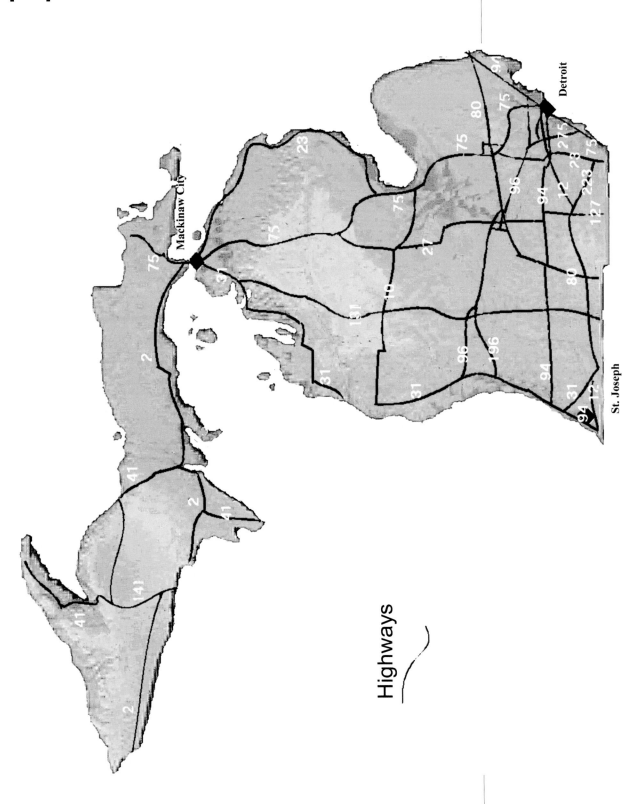

Highways

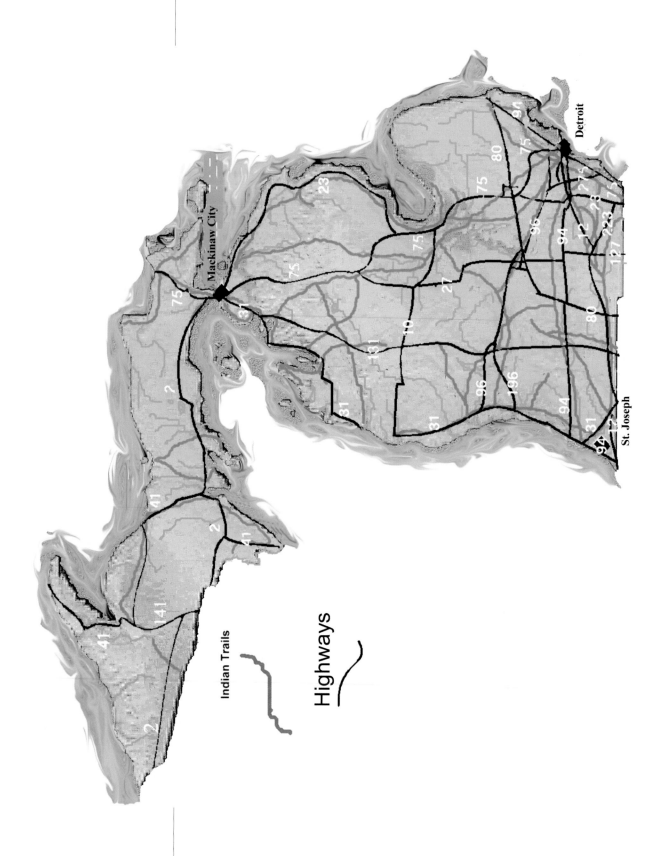

Indian Trails

Highways

 © PATRICK RUSSELL LEBEAU 2005 / ALL RIGHTS RESERVED

COUNTY	INDIAN NAME? (Y/N)	ORIGIN / TRANSLATION
ALCONA County Seat: Harrisville Population: 10,389 Organized: 1869	Schoolcraft invention (i.e., non-Indian)	Believed to be an origination of Henry R. Schoolcraft, who served as mediator between the United States and the Native Americans, and who was also a member of the Territorial Council of Michigan. "Al" is Arabic for "the," "co" means "plain" or "prairie," and "na" means "excellence." Therefore: "a fine or excellent plain."
ALGER County Seat: Munising Population: 9,819 Organized: 1885	No	Named for Governor Russell A. Alger (1885–1886).
ALLEGAN County Seat: Allegan Population: 96,085 Organized: 1835	Schoolcraft invention	A Schoolcraft creation. Allegan is an abbreviation of Allegany. Schoolcraft claims the name originates from "Alligewi," the name of a prehistoric tribe. Other meanings include "lake," "fine river," or "fair river."
ALPENA County Seat: Alpena Population: 30,814 Organized: 1857	Schoolcraft invention	A Schoolcraft creation. Test translation are is "partridge county."
ANTRIM County Name: Bellaire Population: 19,528 Organized 1863	No	Named for County Antrim in Ireland.
ARENAC County Seat: Standish Population: 15,953 Organized: 1883	Yes	A derivation of the Latin "arena" and the Native American "ac." The combined words mean "sandy place."
BARAGA County Seat: L'Anse Population: 8,061 Organized: 1875	No	Named for the missionary Bishop Frederic Baraga (1797–1868).
BARRY County Seat: Hastings Population: 52,231 Organized: 1839	No	Named for William T. Barry (1785–1835) of Kentucky, Postmaster General in the Cabinet of President Andrew Jackson.
BAY CITY County Seat: Bay Population: 111, 772 Organized: 1857	No	So named because it encircles Saginaw Bay.
BENZIE County Seat: Beaulah Population: 13,264 Organized: 1869	No	A derivative of the French "aux-bec-Scies." The name was first applied to the river. It later was changed to Betsey, then to Benzie.
BERRIEN County Seat: St. Joseph Population: 151,734 Organized: 1831	No	Named for John M. Berrien of Georgia, Attorney General under President Jackson.
BRANCH County Seat: Coldwater Population: 41,990 Organized: 1833	No	Named for John Branch of North Carolina, Secretary of the Navy under President Jackson.
CALHOUN County Seat: Marshall Population: 139,991 Organized: 1833	No	Named for Vice President John C. Calhoun (1782–1850).
CASS County Seat: Cassopolis Population: 48,920 Organized: 1829	No	Named for Lewis Cass (1782–1866), second Governor of the Michigan Territory.
CHARLEVOIX County Seat: Charlevoix Population: 22,833 Organized: 1869	No	Named for Pierre F. X. de Charlevoix (1682–1761), a Jesuit missionary.

© PATRICK RUSSELL LEBEAU 2005 / ALL RIGHTS RESERVED

CHEBOYGAN County Seat: Cheboygan Population: 22,471 Organized: 1853		Boygan meaning pipe: Big Pipe.
CHIPPEWA County Seat: Sault Ste. Marie Population: 36,591 Organized: 1871	Yes	Modern residue of Ojibwe or Ojibway. Chippewa is the term used on all Michigan Indian treaties. Many of the Indian reservations in Michigan employ "Chippewa" in their official name.
CLARE County Seat: Harrison Population: 27,589 Organized: 1871	No	Named for County Clare in Ireland.
CLINTON County Seat: St. Johns Population: 60,897 Organized: 1839	No	Named for New York governor Dewitt Clinton (1769–1828), under whose administration the Erie Canal was built.
CRAWFORD County Seat: Grayling Population: 13,387 Organized: 1879	No	Named for Colonel William Crawford, an early settler in Michigan.
DELTA County Seat: Escanaba Population: 38,605 Organized: 1861	No	From the Greek "delta," referring to the triangular shape of the original county which included segments of Menominee, Dickinson, Iron and Marquette Counties.
DICKINSON County Seat: Iron Mountain Population: 27,058 Organized: 1891	No	Named for Don M. Dickinson of Michigan, Postmaster General under President Grover Cleveland during his first term.
EATON County Seat: Charlotte Population: 96,805 Organized: 1837	No	Named for John H. Eaton (1790–1856) of Tennessee, Secretary of War under President Jackson.
EMMET County Seat: Petoskey Population: 27,034 Organized: 1853	No	For the Irish Patriot, Robert Emmet (1778–1803).
GENESEE County Seat: Flint Population: 433,300 Organized: 1836	Yes	A Seneca word meaning "beautiful valley." Named after the valley in western New York State from which many Flint area settlers came.
GLADWIN County Seat: Gladwin Population: 23,937 Organized: 1875	No	Named for Major Henry Gladwin, British commander at Detroit in 1762.
GOGEBIC County Seat: Bessmer Population: 18,016 Organized: 1887	Unknown	An obscure word. Varying references interpret it as "Rock," "Green Lake," "Trembling Ground," and "High Lake."
GRAND TRAVERSE County Seat: Traverse City Population: 69,582 Organized: 1851	No	A French phrase "grande traverse," meaning "long crossing."
GRATIOT County Seat: Ithaca Population: 39,785 Organized: 1855	No	For Captain Charles Gratiot (1788–1855), who supervised the building of Fort Gratiot at the modern site of Port Huron.
HILLSDALE County Seat: Hillsdale Population: 44,829 Organized: 1835	No	The rolling surface of the area served as the basis for this name.
HOUGHTON County Seat: Houghton Population: 36,375 Organized: 1848	No	For Michigan geologist Professor Douglas Houghton (1809–1845).

 © PATRICK RUSSELL LEBEAU 2005 / ALL RIGHTS RESERVED

HURON County Seat: Bad Axe Population: 35,214 Organized: 1859	Yes	Name of a Native American tribe. From the French word "hure," meaning "peasant" or "big (ugly) head." The tribe referred to itself as "Wendat" (Wyandotte), meaning "dwellers on a peninsula."
INGHAM County Seat: Mason Population: 278,423 Organized: 18??	No	Named for Samuel D. Ingham of Pennsylvania, Secretary of the Treasury under President Andrew Jackson.
IONIA County Seat: Ionia Population: 59,193 Organized: 1837	No	For a province in Greece.
IOSCO County Seat: Tawas City Population: 24,034 Organized: 1857	Possible Schoolcraft invention	Possible Schoolcraft invention or the name of a legendary Ottawa hero he writes about in his *Algic Researches* (1839).
IRON County Seat: Crystal Falls Population: 13,131 Organized: 1888?	No	For the mineral product of the county.
ISABELLA County Seat: Mt. Pleasant Population: 57,053 Organized: 1859	No	For Queen Isabella (1451–1504) of Spain.
JACKSON County Seat: Jackson Population: 153,287 Organized: 1832	No	For President Andrew Jackson (1767–1845).
KALAMAZOO County Seat: Kalamazoo Population: 228,796 Organized: 1830	Yes	The most widely accepted translations from Ojibwe are "boiling water," "beautiful water," and "stone like otters." Other versions are "reflecting river" or "it smokes."
KALKASKA County Seat: Kalkaska Population: 14,536 Organized: 1871	Schoolcraft invention	A Schoolcraft creation. Perhaps a combination of Calcraft and Cass. Some sources say the word is derived from Ojibwe for "burned over."
KENT County Seat: Grand Rapids Population: 520,123 Organized: 1836	No	For chancellor James Kent (1763–1817), a celebrated New York jurist.
KEWEENAW County Seat: Eagle River Population: 1,880 Organized: 1861	Yes	Ojibwe word for "portage" or "place where portage is made."
LAKE County Seat: Baldwin Population: 9,631 Organized: 1871	No	The county has many small lakes.
LAPEER County Seat: Lapeer Population: 81,240 Organized: 1835	No	A derivation of the French "La Pierre," meaning stone or flint.
LELANAU County Seat: Leland Population: 18,122 Organized: 1863	Schoolcraft invention	A Schoolcraft creation meaning "delight of life."
LENAWEE County Seat: Adrian Population: 95,661 Organized: 1826	Yes	Shawnee word meaning "man" in the genderless sense, or more properly, "people."
LIVINGSTON County Seat: Howell Population: 129,080 Organized: 1836	No	Named for Edward Livingston (1764–1836) of Louisiana, Secretary of State under President Andrew Jackson.

© PATRICK RUSSELL LEBEAU 2005 / ALL RIGHTS RESERVED

LUCE County Seat: Newberry Population: 5,571 Organized: 1887	No	For Governor Cyrus G. Luce (1887–1890).
MACKINAC County Seat: St. Ignace Population: 10,910 Organized: 1849	Yes	The county was laid out under the name of Fort Michilimackinac in 1818. The fort name signifies "great turtle" while the county name signifies "turtle" in Ojibwa (or a closely related dialect).
MACOMB County Seat: Mt. Clemens Population: 728,563 Organized: 1818	No	For General Alexander Macomb (1782–1841), an officer in the war of 1812.
MANISTEE County Seat: Manistee Population: 22,633 Organized: 1855	Yes	Native American name first applied to the county's principal river. This name has the same origin as that of Manistique which is a derivation from either the Ojibwa word for "crooked river," or the Algonquin for "island all wooded."
MARQUETTE County Seat: Marquette Population: 70,683 Organized: 1846	No	For the Jesuit missionary and explorer, Father Jacques Marquette.
MASON County Seat: Ludington Population: 27,200 Organized: 1855	No	For Stevens T. Mason (1811–1843), first Governor of Michigan (1835–1840).
MECOSTA County Seat: Big Rapids Population: 38,620 Organized: 1859	Yes	For the Potawatomi chief, Mecosta. The name represents "bear club," "little bear" or "young bear" in Ojibwa, Ottawa, and Potawatomi.
MENOMINEE County Seat: Menominee Population: 24,532 Organized: 1861	Yes	Ojibwe derivation of the word means "wild rice people." County named for the Menominee River, which took its name from the tribe that lived in the county.
MIDLAND County Seat: Midland Population: 79,245 Organized: 1850	No	Located near the geographic center of the Lower Peninsula.
MISSAUKEE County Seat: Lake City Population: 13,347 Organized: 1850	Yes	Named for a prominent Ottawa chief of the area who was known better as "Me-sau-kee."
MONROE County Seat: Monroe Population: 137,716 Organized: 1822	No	For President James Monroe (1758–1831).
MONTCALM County Seat: Stanton Population: 56,886 Organized: 1850	No	For the French General, Marquis de Montcalm.
MONTMORENCY County Seat: Atlanta Population: 9,513 Organized: 1881	Unknown	Derivation unknown. Perhaps named for a French explorer or a type of cherry.
MUSKEGON County Seat: Muskegon Population: 163,436 Organized: 1859	Yes	Derived from Ojibwa "maskig" meaning "swamp" or "marsh," and "ong" meaning "place."
NEWAYGO County Seat: White Cloud Population: 42,738 Organized: 1851	Yes	Supposedly named for an Ottawa band chief.

  © PATRICK RUSSELL LEBEAU 2005 / ALL RIGHTS RESERVED

OAKLAND County Seat: Pontiac Population: 1,141,997 Organized: 1820	No	So named because of the abundance of oak trees in the county.
OCEANA County Seat: Hart Population: 23,493 Organized: 1851	No	Derives its name because of its proximity to Lake Michigan.
OGEMAW County Seat: West Branch Population: 20,250 Organized: 1875	Yes	Named after Ogema-kegato (1794–1840), prominent chief of the Saginaw band. Taken from the Ojibwa word for "chief."
ONTONAGON County Seat: Ontonagon Population: 8,673 Organized: 1846	Yes	Various Ojibwa meanings include "hunting river," "lost dish," and "fishing place."
OSCEOLA County Seat: Reed City Population: 21,375 Organized: 1869	Yes	For the Seminole Native American chief, Osceola (1803–1838). Derived from the Creek word "assiyahola," meaning "black drink singer."
OSCODA County Seat: Mio Population: 8,494 Organized: 1881	Schoolcraft invention	Believed to be a combination of two Ojibwa words, created by Schoolcraft from "ossin" (stone or pebble) and "mushcoda" (a prairie or meadow).
OTSEGO County Seat: Gaylord Population: 20,101 Organized: 1875	Yes	Named after a county in New York. The name is related to "Otesaga" translated as "signification lost" or "place of the rock."
OTTAWA County Seat: Grand Haven Population: 205,333 Organized: 1837	Yes	For the Ottawa Native American tribe. Derived from "O-dah-waug," meaning "trading people."
PRESQUE ISLE County Seat: Rogers City Population: 14,028 Organized: 1871	No	A derivation of the French phrase for "narrow peninsula" or "almost an island."
ROSCOMMON County Seat: Roscommon Population: 21,881 Organized: 1875	No	For County Roscommon, Ireland.
SAGINAW County Seat: Saginaw Population: 211,287 Organized: 1831	Yes	There are two known derivations. "Sac-e-nong" (Sauk Town), because the Sauk Indians once occupied the area. The other possible meaning comes from the Ojibwa words "saging" or "saginang" for "at the mouth of the river."
ST. CLAIR County Seat: Port Huron Population: 152,351 Organized: 1821	No	For General Arthur St. Clair, first Governor of the Northwest Territory.
ST. JOSEPH County Seat: Centreville Population: 59,999 Organized: 1829	No	For the patron saint of New France.
SANILAC County Seat: Sandusky Population: 41,567 Organized: 1848	Possible Schoolcraft invention	Possibly for Sannilac, a spirit warrior in Henry Whiting's poem Sannilac. An artificial name with no roots in either Algonquian or Iroquoian languages. However, may have been obtained from Governor Cass' manuscripts.
SCHOOLCRAFT County Seat: Manistique Population: 8,596 Organized: 1846	No	For Henry R. Schoolcraft, Michigan's Native American agent.

© PATRICK RUSSELL LEBEAU 2005 / ALL RIGHTS RESERVED

SHIAWASSEE County Seat: Corunna Population: 71,644 Organized: 1837	Yes	Named for Shiawassee River. Meaning usually believed to signify "the river that twists about" or "it runs back and forwards." Other possible meanings are "straight ahead water" or "straight running river."
TUSCOLA County Seat: Caro Population: 57,017 Organized: 1850	Schoolcraft invention	A Schoolcraft creation meaning either "warrior prairie" or "level lands."
VAN BUREN County Seat: Paw Paw Population: 73,848 Organized: 1837	No	For President Martin Van Buren, who was inaugurated in 1837.
WASHTENAW County Seat: Ann Arbor Population: 290,542 Organized: 1829	Yes	The original Ojibwa word was "wash-ten-ong" meaning "on the river."
WAYNE County Seat: Detroit Population: 2,064,908 Organized: 1815	No	For General Anthony Wayne (1745–1796), who became famous in the Revolutionary War through his courageous exploits.
WEXFORD County Seat: Cadillac Population: 28,115 Organized: 1869	No	For County Wexford, Ireland.

© PATRICK RUSSELL LEBEAU 2005 / ALL RIGHTS RESERVED

[4.23] INDIAN PLACE-NAMES IN MICHIGAN: WORKSHEET

Choose 10 to 13 county names and guess which are of Indian origin. If you guess that it is *not* an Indian name, guess its origin. Work with your fellow students and teacher to discover the origin and/or the translation of the county names.

COUNTY	INDIAN NAME? [Y/N]	ORIGIN / TRANSLATION

© PATRICK RUSSELL LEBEAU 2005 / ALL RIGHTS RESERVED

Henry Schoolcraft (1789–1865) was born in New York State but spent most of his life on Michigan's frontier. He worked for nearly 20 years as an agent to the Chippewa at Sault Ste. Marie and Mackinaw. He married Jane Johnson, a granddaughter of Chief Wabojeeg and was a member of the Michigan territorial legislature from 1828–32. It was during this time that he introduced legislation creating a system of county and township names for Michigan.

Schoolcraft named 32 Michigan county names that are wholly or partly drawn from Indian or allegedly Indian names. Many of the names he proposed, names with Arabic prefixes, and suffixes from Latin, French, and English. For example, his frequent use of the prefix *al* is sometimes intended to represent the Arabic article, and at other times it stands for the first syllable of Algonquian.

Great Lake States with Indian Names

Illinois	From the Illini Indian word meaning "men" or "warriors," supplemented by the French adjective ending *ois*.
Indiana	The word presumably comes from the fact that the land lying along the Ohio River was purchased from the Indians. Others claim it was named for the Indian tribes who settled in western Pennsylvania.
Michigan	The word comes from the Algonquian word *Mishagamaw* meaning "big lake" or "great water." It is also said to be from *Michi* meaning "great" and *Gama* meaning "water."
Minnesota	The word comes from the Sioux word meaning "cloudy water" or "sky tinted water"; derived its name from the river of the same name.
Ohio	The Iroquois Indian word means "beautiful river," taken from the river of the same name.
Wisconsin	This word is believed to be an Indian name whose meaning is uncertain. The state was named after its principal river, which is said to mean "wild rushing channel" or "holes in the banks of the stream in which birds nest." It was spelled *Ouiconsin* and *Misconsing* by early chroniclers.

 © PATRICK RUSSELL LEBEAU 2005 / ALL RIGHTS RESERVED

© PATRICK RUSSELL LEBEAU 2005 / ALL RIGHTS RESERVED

KEWEENAW

HOUGHTON

ONTONAGON

GOGEBIC

BARAGA

IRON

MARQUETTE

LUCE

SCHOOL-
CRAFT

CHIPPEWA

ALGER

DICKINSON

MACKINAC

DELTA

MEN-
OMINEE

EMMET

CHE-
BOYGAN

PRESQUE
ISLE

CHARLE-
VOIX

OTSEGO

MONTMOR-
ENCY

ALPENA

ANTRIM

LEE-
LANAU

KALKASKA

CRAWFORD

OSCODA

ALCONA

BENZIE

GRAND
TRAVERSE

MANISTEE

WEXFORD

MISSAUKEE

ROSCOMMON

OGEMAW

IOSCO

MASON

LAKE

OSCEOLA

CLARE

GLADWIN

ARENAC

HURON

OCEANA

NEWAYGO

MECOSTA

ISABELLA

MIDLAND

BAY

TUSCOLA

SANILAC

MUSKE-
GON

KENT

MONTCALM

GRATIOT

SAGINAW

OTTAWA

IONIA

CLINTON

SHIA-
WASSEE

GENESEE

LAPEER

ST. CLAIR

OAKLAND

MACOMB

ALLEGAN

BARRY

EATON

INGHAM

LIVINGSTON

VAN BUREN

KALAMA-
ZOO

CALHOUN

JACKSON

WASHTENAW

WAYNE

CASS

ST. JOSEPH

BRANCH

HILLSDALE

LENAWEE

MONROE

BERRIEN

Indian word or person
Schoolcraft creation
French word
Person (non-Indian)
Place
Other

© PATRICK RUSSELL LEBEAU 2005 / ALL RIGHTS RESERVED

Indian Treaty Land Cessions

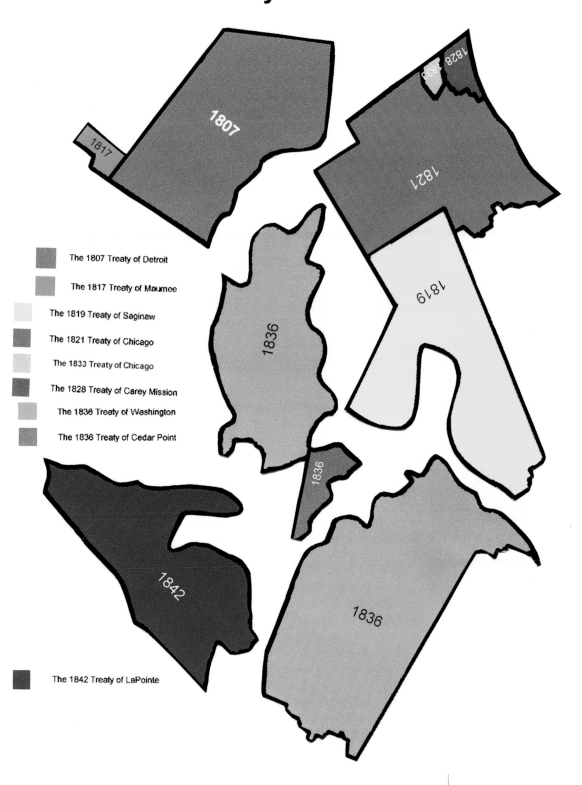

The 1807 Treaty of Detroit

The 1817 Treaty of Maumee

The 1819 Treaty of Saginaw

The 1821 Treaty of Chicago

The 1833 Treaty of Chicago

The 1828 Treaty of Carey Mission

The 1836 Treaty of Washington

The 1836 Treaty of Cedar Point

The 1842 Treaty of LaPointe

© PATRICK RUSSELL LEBEAU 2005 / ALL RIGHTS RESERVED

Indian Treaty Land Cessions

1807

1817

1819

1821

1836

1836

1828 1833

1842

1836

The 1807 Treaty of Detroit

The 1817 Treaty of Maumee

The 1819 Treaty of Saginaw

The 1821 Treaty of Chicago

The 1828 Treaty of Carey Mission

The 1833 Treaty of Chicago

The 1836 Treaty of Washington

The 1836 Treaty of Cedar Point

The 1842 Treaty of LaPointe

© PATRICK RUSSELL LEBEAU 2005 / ALL RIGHTS RESERVED

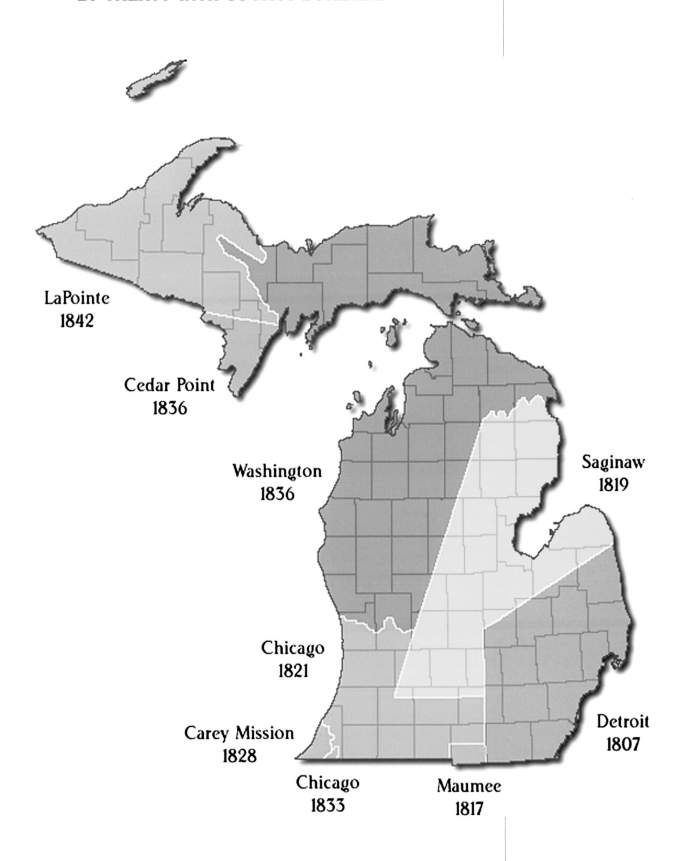

LaPointe
1842

Cedar Point
1836

Washington
1836

Saginaw
1819

Chicago
1821

Carey Mission
1828

Detroit
1807

Chicago
1833

Maumee
1817

© PATRICK RUSSELL LEBEAU 2005 / ALL RIGHTS RESERVED

1795	Treaty of Greenville, Ohio (*not shown*)
1807	Treaty of Detroit, Michigan
1809	Act of Congress (*not shown*)
1817	Treaty of Miami of Lake Erie
1818	Treaty of St. Mary's, Ohio (*not shown*)
1819	Treaty of Saginaw, Michigan territory
1820	Treaty of Michillimackinac (*not shown*)
1821	Treaty of Chicago, Illinois
1827	Treaty of St. Joseph, Michigan Territory (*not shown*)
1828	Treaty of St. Joseph River
1832	Treaty of Tippecanoe River, Indiana (*not shown*)
1833	Treaty of Chicago, Illinois
1836	Treaty of Washington, D.C. (March 28)
1836	Treaty of Washington, D.C. (May 9) (*not shown*)
1836	Treaty of Cedar Pointe, Wisconsin Territory
1837	Treaty of Detroit, Michigan
1842	Treaty of LaPointe, Wisconsin Territory

References

Dunbar, Willis Frederick, *Michigan: A History of the Wolverine State* (Grand Rapids: William B. Eerdmans Publishing, 1970), p. 44 (modified).

Powell, J. W., ed., *Eighteenth Annual report of the Bureau of American Ethnology to the Secretary of the Smithsonian Institution, 1896–97*, part 2, *Schedule of Indian Land Cessions* (Washington: U.S. Government Printing office, 1899), pp. 654–796. Powell's report, including a detailed map (plate 136), identified seventeen treaties in which Native American tribes ceded land in Michigan and surrounding states. Ten of the major cessions are shown here; the remainder either involved very small areas or areas that were also included in subsequent cessions.

 © PATRICK RUSSELL LEBEAU 2005 / ALL RIGHTS RESERVED

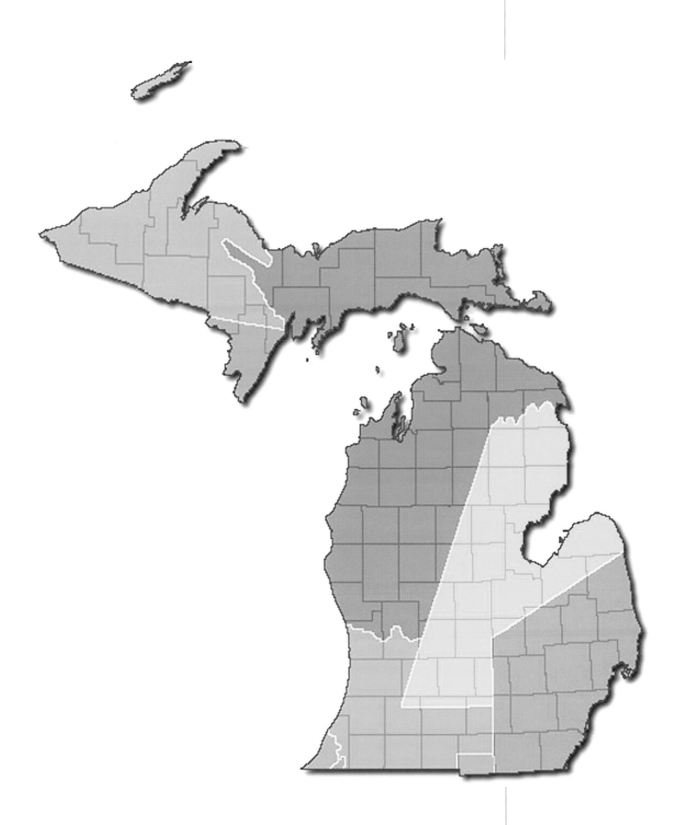

© PATRICK RUSSELL LEBEAU 2005 / ALL RIGHTS RESERVED

The Ojibwa people have a rich oral and pictorial tradition regarding their origins and migration from the Atlantic Ocean westward through the St. Lawrence Valley and the Great Lakes to Wisconsin and Minnesota. The tale of this journey over thousands of miles many hundreds of years ago is vivid and full of myths of good and evil spirits. There are many versions of the migration, all focusing on the travels of a bear and otter, who were carefully chosen by the Manito Council to take westward the teachings of the MidéWiwin, or Grand Medicine Society, which was organized to teach the great rules of proper life. The journey was often recorded on birch bark scrolls, and one abstraction of the journey is shown here. The modern map of eastern North America shows the geographic path of the journey, and the following story tells the colorful tale that coincides with this bark scroll migration path.

While written in the symbolism of mythology, the maps of the ancient migration of the Ojibwa have identifiable reference points to the modern landscape. A careful study of the Red Sky map as well as several other birch bark migration maps permits the accurate plotting of the legendary journey from the Great Salt Sea to Minnesota's Leech Lake. This route and places of great mythological significance are shown on today's map of the Great Lakes region.

The Story of the Migration as Told by James Red Sky

(Eshkway Keezhik) to Selwyn Dewdney

After the Great Manito or God had created all creatures on earth, he found that they were dying off and decided he needed to get them to worship him, but he didn't know how. So he called a meeting of all the birds and all the creatures on earth to talk about it, "somewhere across the Big Water, where this Manito was." The Manito needed someone to take his message to the people and asked who would do it. The Bear was there and said, "I'll take it across to the people." The Bear went off with the message of Everlasting Life, but it was very heavy to carry, and he could barely walk. When he came to a wall, he couldn't get through it at first until he stuck his tongue out, which made a little hole that he could get through. He did this each time he came to a wall, and the four wind Manitos stationed at each of the cardinal directions thanked him for the work he did. He came upon four walls before he finally got through to Midéwegun or Midélodge. The Bear had successfully carried the Pack of Life this far when he met the Megis, the Shell, who took over the trek down the St. Lawrence River to Montreal, past the Lachine Rapids to Mattawa,

© PATRICK RUSSELL LEBEAU 2005 / ALL RIGHTS RESERVED

on down the French River to Lake Huron, through the Straits of Mackinac to Sault Ste. Marie. Somewhere along the stretch of the journey, the Megis transferred the Pack of Life to the Otter, who carried it along the south shore of Lake Superior and up the St. Louis River west to Leech Lake. All along the way, Midé centers were established to teach the way of the great rules of life. The Otter had to pass the malevolent underwater spirits Mis-shi-pe-shu and Mi-shi-nah-may-gway and follow the route of the sacred portage. From here the Otter went to the East Savannah River, where another portage had to be made to Big Sandy Lake, then to the Mississippi River, where two "wrong" rivers are depicted as snakes. A short journey up the Mississippi to its headwaters by the Otter revealed no Indian villages, so he came back down and continued his journey west until he arrived at Leech Lake in Minnesota, where a Midé center was established.

This information is taken from an exhibit at the Museum of Ojibwa Culture, St. Ignace, Michigan. Used with permission.

Can you find the particular "word pictures" depicted on the chart? Can you create your own word pictures to tell a personal story of an adventure or journey? Can you create a chart of your family history?

Ge-wah-ni-chee-gay ze-bee, or "wrong rivers," on the journey are shown as lakes, an explicit reference to evil sorcery and the dangers of misusing special powers.

O-gee-jok (Crane) drawings appear on many migration charts inside the bounds of Lake Superior. A Nett Lake man explains the mythological and historical role of the crane: "The crane is the bird-god that lives in the heavens. He pays special attention to the supplications of man. The fire of his eyes will last forever. His eye is the sun."

Ne-gig (Otter) is a messenger sent by the Manito Council to take the Pack of Life, which contained all the great rules of life, on the journey.

Ma-kwa (Bear) is shown by a figure of a bear, by his path shown by his paw print, or by a stylized representation of his tongue or head. The Bear also carried messages for the Manito Council.

Mis-she-pe-shu (Great Lynx or Underwater Panther) is a superior Manito. He lives in the Under-Earth and controls the water of lakes, rivers, and streams. He causes great waves, whirlpools, and non-navigable currents by repeatedly striking the water with his powerful tail. This allegorical creature incorporates the daily fears of Ojibwa people, who traveled primarily by water routes and consequently realized the dangers of summer squalls and frozen winter waters.

Mis-shi-nah-may-gway (Huge Fish Monster) is a malevolent spirit combining an evil snake and a whale-like fish with a human head. He guards waterways and requires offerings before allowing safe passage. The perpendicular squiggly lines represent a branch of the Upper Mississippi River flowing out of the north from its headwaters. The particular undulations indicate where the Otter went up the Mississippi River, could not find any Indian villages, and came back.

Megis is a cowrie shell discussed in Ojibwa mythology and medicine ceremonies. The Ojibwa forefathers originally found it at the Great Water (Atlantic Ocean). The Megis later showed the Ojibwa elders the pathway westward and helped carry the Pack of Life containing rules for good living, as depicted in this migration map.

 © PATRICK RUSSELL LEBEAU 2005 / ALL RIGHTS RESERVED

[4.34] OJIBWA MIGRATION CHART

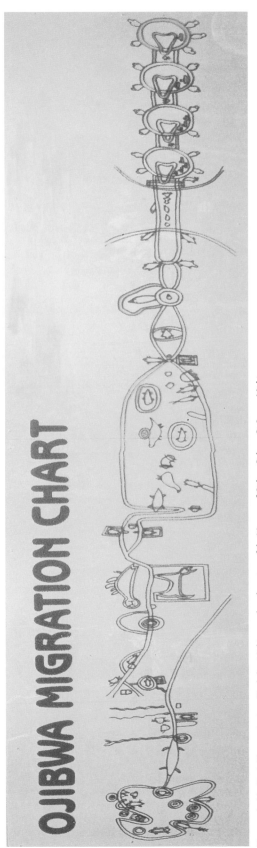

OJIBWA MIGRATION CHART

Photographed by Davie Communications, Kincheloe, Michigan, and used courtesy of the Museum of Ojibwa Culture, St. Ignace, Michigan.

© PATRICK RUSSELL LEBEAU 2005 / ALL RIGHTS RESERVED

© PATRICK RUSSELL LEBEAU 2005 / ALL RIGHTS RESERVED

© PATRICK RUSSELL LEBEAU 2005 / ALL RIGHTS RESERVED

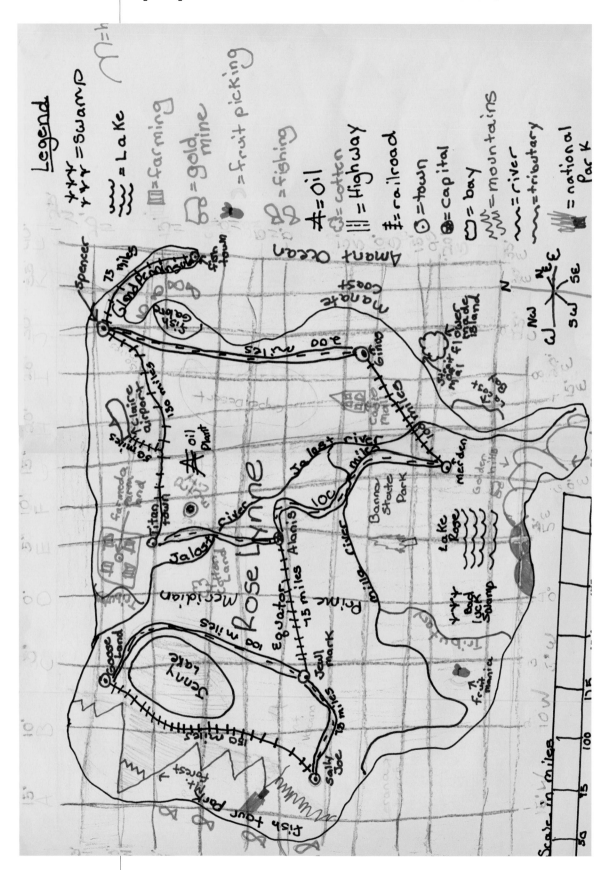

© PATRICK RUSSELL LEBEAU 2005 / ALL RIGHTS RESERVED

[4.38] QUESTIONS FOR THOUGHT AND DISCUSSION
▶ LESSON THE FOURTH

Activity A ▶ Finding Michigan Indian Villages, circa 1760

① Why are the villages located near rivers or the shorelines of the Great Lakes?

② What is the Seven Years War most often called in U.S. history books?

③ Because (4.1) is based on a map created before the Seven Years War, what language is the map written in?

④ Can you identify or describe the relative locations where the Ottawas, Potawatomis, and Chippewas lived?

⑤ Do the relative locations of Indian population correspond to your understanding of where they live now?

Activity B ▶ Examining the Schoolcraft Map of 1837

① Do you think Schoolcraft's "reservations" look too large for the relative population of 8,000 Indians in 1837 and too small for the relative population of 56,000 in 1990?

② For 1837, would you say Michigan Indians lived in relatively rural or isolated areas? How many major cities are shown on the map?

③ In a very basic estimate, what percentage of Michigan land is set aside for Indians? What percentage is set aside for American settlement?

④ Why was Schoolcraft required to make a map of Michigan Indian land cessions, of Indian populations, and of the size and location of reserved lands?

Activity C ▶ Finding the Relative Locations of Indian Reservations in 2000 and Comparing Them to Schoolcraft's Locations in 1837

① Consider the official titles and disregard the use of the noun *Indian* for now. What is the relevance of the other terms used—for example, *Bay Mills, Little Traverse Bay*, and *Saginaw?*

② Comment on the significance of the words *community* and *band*. Use a dictionary to get a start.

③ Why is *Indian* used?

④ Notice the use of *Chippewa, Odawa* and *Ottawa*, and *Potawatomi*. Also notice that some "communities" only use the term *Indian*. What do all these designations imply?

⑤ Do Indian reservations exist within counties with major cities, such as Wayne County (Detroit), Genesee County (Flint), or Kent County (Grand

© PATRICK RUSSELL LEBEAU 2005 / ALL RIGHTS RESERVED

Rapids)? Does the location of Indian reservations suggest isolation? Or rural? Perhaps exotic? Explain.

⑥ What comparisons can you make between the 2000 map "Federally Recognized American Indian Tribes" (4.3) and Schoolcraft's 1837 map (4.2)? Are the locations similar? Compare both to the "Relative Positions" map of 1760 (4.1). Are locations similar? What does the relative position of Indian communities between the maps suggest about consistency over time? How have the names of the Indian communities changed over time?

Activity D ▶ Exploring the Location of Indian Casinos

① Closely examine "American Indian and Other Casinos, circa 2000" (4.5), and "Comparison of Locator Map to Casino Map" (4.6). Where are casinos located?

② Do most of the casinos correspond to the locations of Indian reservations? Why might this relationship exist?

③ The slot machine symbol used to locate Indian casinos is exaggerated for emphasis. What is that emphasis?

④ How can casinos help you to locate Indian reservations? Can casinos help you to understand the concepts of reserved rights and sovereignty? Explain.

Activity E ▶ Mapping Michigan's Native American Population Using Schoolcraft's 1837 Map and U.S. Census Data: Graduated Circle Mapping

① What areas of Michigan have the highest concentration of Indian people? Do these areas correspond to the areas of Indian population today? What are the differences?

② In what areas are there no Indians?

③ Where are Indians located? Can you give any geographical information for why Indians might be located in specific places?

④ How evenly or equally is the Indian population distributed around Michigan? In comparison to the choropleth exercise, do you find this distribution today? What are the differences?

⑤ How do the "reserved lands" or "reservations" (the shaded areas on Schoolcraft's map) correspond to the location of Indian people? If the reservations can accommodate population, can the reservations accommodate distribution (the many places Indians live)? Are the reservations too cramped or restrictive? Why or why not?

⑥ Reservations are indicated on the Schoolcraft map. Do reservations exist today in the areas you mapped? Use (4.3) and (4.4) to decide.

⑦ Look closely at (4.10). What does this map tell you about the locations of Indian population? Does this map clarify distribution? ([4.16] may help here as well.)

 © PATRICK RUSSELL LEBEAU 2005 / ALL RIGHTS RESERVED

⑧ In comparison to the general graduating circle mapping, in particular the use of various sizes of circles, how is this map better at indicating the locations of Indian populations?

Activity E ▶ Mapping Michigan's Native American Population Using Schoolcraft's 1837 Map and U.S. Census Data: Choropleth Mapping

① Which counties have the highest Indian population? What are the relative locations of those counties?

② Which counties have the highest percentage of Indians? What are the relative locations of those counties?

③ Notice that the counties in questions 1 and 2 are not the necessarily the same. What are the differences?

④ Why do so many Indians live in urban counties?

⑤ Why do so many rural counties have a high percentage of Indians?

⑥ Using (4.4), compare the land areas involved in different Michigan Indian treaties with current Indian populations. What connections do you see or not see? What connections did you expect to see but didn't?

⑦ Using (4.4), locate present-day reservations. How does the presence of a reservation affect a county's percentage of Indian population?

Part 2 ▶ Relationships and Movement within Places: Michigan's Indians Interacting with the Michigan Landscape and Environment and the Influence of Indian Place-Names

Activity A ▶ Forts and Cities

① Why are forts located where they are? How are they accessed?

② What are forts used for? Whom are they meant to protect?

③ Forts are the initial locations of Euro-American settlement. Most historical maps used in public school classrooms do not indicate Indian settlements. Why not?

④ According to (4.1), (4.15), and (4.16), are forts located near Indian settlements? Why or why not?

⑤ What cities are now located where forts used to be? What city is the most prominent (has the greatest population)? Explain.

Activity B ▶ Indian Trails in Michigan

① Why do you think the Michigan Indians chose to use their routes over and over again?

② Why do you think there are more trails in the Detroit area?

③ Where are trails located in the Upper Peninsula? Why fewer trails in the Upper Peninsula?

④ Study (4.1) and (4.2). How do Indian trails correspond to the locations of Indian populations in 1760 and 1837? Are the locations of Indian populations connected by trails?

⑤ List as many observations you can make about Indian trails in Michigan.

Activity C ▶ Waterways, Highways, and Byways

① Compare the Indian trails on (4.18) with the locations of rivers and major waterways on (4.19). What observations do you have now?

② Study (4.1) and (4.2). How do major waterways correspond to the locations of Indian populations in 1760 and 1837? Are the locations of Indian population connected by waterways (rivers and lakes)?

③ In 1760 and 1837, how do Indians travel by water? What is their mode of transportation?

④ Why do you think Indian trails eventually became roads and highways?

⑤ How would the Indians of today use roads and highways? What would be their purpose?

⑥ Study (4.15). How would Indians travel to Michigan's major cities? Why would they make this trip?

⑦ Using (4.21), what are the relationships between Indian trails, water routes, and highways?

Activity D ▶ Indian Place-Names in Michigan

① Did it seem easy or difficult to identify Indian-named places? Why do you think it was easy/difficult?

② If you could rename your town, what would you rename it and why?

③ Does the name given to a place have a relationship to the location of the place? Give an example.

④ Do any of the Indian names make sense in terms of the location of Indian villages, reservations, or population concentrations?

⑤ How many counties are named after Indian warriors? Are these Indian warriors from Michigan?

⑥ How many counties are named for Indian people? Are these people Michigan Indians?

⑦ Some of the names are pseudo-Indian names, meaning they are meant to sound-like or represent Indian language but are inventions. Henry Schoolcraft invented most of these names, like Alcona. Did you mark *yes* on the worksheet for a county you later learned was a Schoolcraft invention? If so, why? Is the yes answer correct? Explain. How are these inventions believable?

 © PATRICK RUSSELL LEBEAU 2005 / ALL RIGHTS RESERVED

8. Can you invent your own "Indian-sounding" name? How easy/difficult is this task?

9. Why name states with Indian words or parts of words?

10. Was it easy for your classmate to follow your directions? How could you have written them better to make them easier to follow?

Part 3 ▶ How Michigan's Land Cession Treaties and Indian Reservations Create Unique Regions within the State

Activity A ▶ How Maps Show Treaties as Land Acquisition Instruments and State-Building Documents

1. How many years did it take for Michigan to become a state?

2. After the March 28, 1836 Treaty of Washington, enough Indian land (the whole Lower Peninsula) had been acquired to create the state of Michigan. Why could treaty negotiators go ahead with statehood without the western portion of the Upper Peninsula?

3. What is the general direction (or flow) of treaties and land acquisition. East to west? Southeast to northwest? What does this flow of land acquisition reveal about how American history is taught?

4. Is the general image of American history an east to west progression? Why or why not?

Activity B ▶ Native American Land Cessions by Treaty and County Borders: How Maps Create Borders

1. How many major land cession treaties are they? How many years does the treaty-making process take?

2. How are lands legally acquired? What is the first step in the state-building process?

3. Why are treaties necessary? Why not just take the land? What legal foundation do treaties establish?

4. Name the four treaties that acquired the most land for state-building purposes. What one treaty acquired the most land? When did Michigan become a state? Explain any relationships or connections between treaties and state building.

Activity C ▶ County Borders and the Birth of a State: A Short Test of Knowledge

1. Find the county in which you live and name the treaty or treaties that enabled the county to be created.

2. Why are counties an important part (or component) of states? What political, social, or economic purpose do counties serve? Like land cessions and treaties, are counties building blocks of states? How?

© PATRICK RUSSELL LEBEAU 2005 / ALL RIGHTS RESERVED

③ Name the four major land cession treaties on (4.31). Name all nine for additional credit. If you'd like, color-code the treaties as you identify them.

Part 4 ▶ Different Ways of Mapping Culture and History

Activity A ▶ Reading/Responding to the Ojibwa Migration Story

① The "Ojibwa Migration Chart" (4.34) flows east to west. How are water or waterways depicted? Why are rivers and lakes important to the migration?

② Can you find the "wrong rivers," "Crane," "Bear," and "Otter"?

③ Compare the Story of Migration to the chart itself. Are they the same? Is there more information on the chart or in the words? How can there be more information on the chart?

④ How would you create your own maps of journeys and travels (imagined or real)? What would be most important to you, and how would you symbolize that importance?

⑤ How can maps such as the migration chart help a person remember important events or knowledge?

⑥ How does the chart depict a moral environment? How does the Pack of Life create a human geography?

Activity B ▶ The Great and Powerful Shoemaker: How Shoes Reveal Cultural Knowledge

① How is "The Great and Powerful Shoemaker" a map? What information does it convey?

② How do the shoes tell a story about our culture or our society?

Activity C ▶ Student Example: Mapping an Original Story or Journey

① How was your story interpreted? Were others able to "read" your story?

② Did you use images or symbols others could recognize? Could you have used more recognizable symbols? If so, what kind, and how would they fit into your story?

③ When you added words (when you explained your depiction), did others have a greater understanding of your intent?

④ How does your pictograph help you to remember an important event or time in your life?

⑤ What is most important about your story, and how is it emphasized in your map?

 © PATRICK RUSSELL LEBEAU 2005 / ALL RIGHTS RESERVED

Activity D ► Creating a Map of a Meaningful Place

1. How are the maps produced in these activities related to the conventional maps? How do these maps differ?

2. What have you learned about historical maps?

3. What is the importance of personal maps, such as the ones created in this lesson, or maps specific to Indian culture?

© PATRICK RUSSELL LEBEAU 2005 / ALL RIGHTS RESERVED

Selected Instructional/Research Resources for Teachers

HISTORY

Blackbird, Andrew J. *History of the Ottawa and Chippewa Indians of Michigan: A Grammar of Their Language and Personal and Family History of the Author*, 1887; reprint, Petoskey, Mich.: Little Traverse Regional Historical Society, 1967. This is a personal narrative history of Cross Village, Middle Village, and Good Hart, Michigan. It includes moral commandments.

Bussey, M. T., and Simon Otto. *Aube Na Bing: A Pictorial History of Michigan Indians, 1865–1988*. Grand Rapids: Michigan Indian Press, 1989. The title of this book means "looking back." It is an important compilation of photographs from personal and archival collections. The book provides a photographic documentary of the Michigan tribes' culture and lifeways. It is an excellent classroom aid and a visual insight into the history of Michigan's Native American community.

Clifton, James. *The Pokagons, 1683–1983: Catholic Potawatomi Indians of the St. Joseph River Valley*. New York: University Press of America, 1984. This is an ethnohistorical reconstruction of the Pokagon Band of Potawatomis in southwestern Michigan. The book provides a rich description of Potawatomi history, culture, and interaction with the U.S. government and citizens.

Densmore, Frances. *Chippewa Customs*. Minneapolis: Ross and Haines, 1970. This book covers many aspects of Ojibwa life, including dwellings, clothing, food, treatment of the sick, care of infants, and much more.

Johnston, Basil. *Ojibway Ceremonies*. Toronto: McClelland and Stewart, 1982. This glimpse of Ojibway culture before its disruption by Europeans is provided in story form, preserving the attitudes and beliefs of the Ojibway. Johnston focuses on a young member of the tribe and his development through participation in the many rituals important to the Ojibway way of life, including the Naming Ceremony, the Vision Quest, the Way Path, the Marriage Ceremony, and the Ritual of the Dead.

Tanner, Helen E., ed. *The Atlas of Great Lakes Indians*. New York: Rand McNally, 1986. This book focuses on Great Lakes Native Americans and their lands in eastern Michigan and Ohio from 1400 to 1873.

HISTORICAL FICTION

Broker, Ignatia. *Night Flying Woman: An Ojibway Narrative.* St. Paul: Minnesota Historical Press, 1983. This wonderful story covers the life of Nibowiseque (Night Flying Woman) from her birth in 1860 until 1942. Night Flying Woman's story offers a glimpse into the changes in Ojibway life over that time, a period that covers the early transition of the Ojibway people from their precontact existence to postcontact reservation and boarding-school life.

Traver, Robert. *Laughing Whitefish.* New York: McGraw-Hill, 1965. This book is based on an actual case fought bitterly in the Michigan courts nearly a hundred years ago. Traver provides a vibrant Victorian courtroom drama, a tender romance, and a wonderful re-creation of the times, the people, and the mores. The case focuses on the rights of the daughter of Marji Kawbawgam to collect the debt owed to her father by the rich Jackson Ore Company. *Note:* This story includes language representative of the times but very uncomfortable in today's settings, such as referring to an Indian woman as a *squaw.* The language and issues should be discussed with young readers as this story is read.

MODERN FICTION

Slipperjack, Ruby. *Honor the Sun.* Winnipeg: Pemmican, 1987. This is a story about a young Native American girl, nicknamed Owl, on an isolated northern Ontario reservation between 1962 and 1968. The story is written as a seasonal diary beginning when Owl is ten years old and is very representative of the experiences of many Native people of that era who grew up on U.S. or Canadian reservations.

REFERENCE READING

Hirschfelder, Arlene, and Martha Kreipe de Montaño. *The Native American Almanac: A Portrait of Native America Today.* New York: Prentice Hall General Reference, 1993. Comprehensive, authoritative, and timely, this book provides a wide-ranging portrait of America's indigenous peoples, combining information about their history and traditions with insight into the topics that most affect their lives today. From the upheaval of first contacts to the policies of removal to contemporary issues of self-determination, this useful sourcebook provides information on all aspects of Native American life.

EDUCATORS' RESOURCES

Hirschfelder, Arlene. *American Indian Stereotypes in the World of Children: A Reader and Bibliography*. Metuchen, N.J.: Scarecrow, 1982. This book presents evidence from a variety of sources, such as advertisements, toys, and pageants, that demonstrates the pervasiveness of the problem of negative stereotyping.

Seale, Doris, Beverly Slapin, and Carolyn Silverman. *Thanksgiving: A Native Perspective*. Berkeley, Calif.: Oyate Press, 1998. A collection of writings from various Native and non-Native sources recounting an accurate history of the time. In addition, the book includes topical writings.

Slapin, Beverly, and Doris Seale, eds. *Through Indian Eyes: The Native Experience in Books for Children*. Philadelphia: New Society, 1992. For educators, parents, librarians, and anyone else interested in responsible multicultural education, this book offers nine essays (eight of them by Native American writers) that confront the impact of stereotyping on children. The collection contains poetry, art, and stories by Native Americans. More than a hundred short reviews critique children's books on Native Americans. The resource section includes an extensive bibliography of recommended children's books and a resource section on Native American publishers. This useful sourcebook provides information on all aspects of Native American life.